Partnering with Culturally and Linguistically Diverse Families in Special Education

Partnering with Culturally and Linguistically Diverse Families in Special Education

Kristin Vogel-Campbell

ROWMAN & LITTLEFIELD
Lanham • Boulder • New York • London

Associate Acquisitions Editor: Courtney Packard
Assistant Acquisitions Editor: Sarah Rinehart
Sales and Marketing Inquiries: textbooks@rowman.com

Published by Rowman & Littlefield
An imprint of The Rowman & Littlefield Publishing Group, Inc
4501 Forbes Boulevard, Suite 200, Lanham, Maryland 20706
www.rowman.com

86-90 Paul Street, London EC2A 4NE

Copyright © 2024 by The Rowman & Littlefield Publishing Group, Inc.

All rights reserved. No part of this book may be reproduced in any form or by any electronic or mechanical means, including information storage and retrieval systems, without written permission from the publisher, except by a reviewer who may quote passages in a review.

British Library Cataloguing in Publication Information Available

Library of Congress Cataloging-in-Publication Data

Names: Vogel-Campbell, Kristin, author.
Title: Partnering with culturally and linguistically diverse families in special education / Kristin Vogel-Campbell.
Description: Lanham : Rowman & Littlefield, [2024] | Includes bibliographical references and index. | Summary: "Utilizing first-hand accounts of parent and caregiver experiences as they navigate the often-complicated process of Special Education services for their children, this book contributes to the small but significant body of work that centers the voices of parents and caregivers of students with cultural or linguistic differences"—Provided by publisher.
Identifiers: LCCN 2023030223 (print) | LCCN 2023030224 (ebook) | ISBN 9781538180358 (cloth) | ISBN 9781538180365 (paperback) | ISBN 9781538180372 (epub)
Subjects: LCSH: Special education—Parent participation—United States—Case studies. | Children with disabilities—Education—United States—Case studies. | Multicultural education—United States.
Classification: LCC LC4031 .V64 2023 (print) | LCC LC4031 (ebook) | DDC 371.9--dc23/eng/20231024
LC record available at https://lccn.loc.gov/2023030223
LC ebook record available at https://lccn.loc.gov/202303022

Contents

Acknowledgments   vii

PART I • ISSUES IN PARENTAL ENGAGEMENT

1   **Introduction**   3
2   **Literature Review**   15
3   **Theoretical Frameworks**   29

PART II • PARENT NARRATIVES

4   **Emily, Eiko and James, and Leticia**   45
5   **Roger, Gloria and Tony, and Tomas**   65
6   **Lisa and Vanessa**   95
7   **Judi, Aida, and Rachel**   111
8   **Possibilities**   137

     Appendix A: *Methodology*   159
     Appendix B: *Acronym Glossary*   169
     Appendix C: *Parent Dialogue Protocol*   173

References   175
Index   185
About the Author   195

Acknowledgments

Throughout the process of first completing my doctorate and then writing this book, I have had the support of countless family, friends, colleagues, and mentors.

Researching, writing, and defending a dissertation in the midst of a global pandemic is an accomplishment I share with a select cohort of individuals. My critical friends, Drs. Katy Duffy-Sherr and Dung Kim Nguyễn, were instrumental in helping me to cross that finish line. Our weekly Zoom writing sessions were motivating, as were their texts and hilarious memes. I am also appreciative to the entire Department of Educational Leadership teaching staff at California State University, East Bay, especially Drs. Mariama Gray, Kathryn Strom, and Peg Winkelman, my dissertation chair. Dr. Michael Milliken, Karen Breslow, and John Bartfield, thank you for your leadership and mentorship in my work in San Mateo County. My San Mateo Foster City colleagues past and present, I am grateful to be able to thought partner with you and work for equity for our students.

Thank you to Chris Holland for the assets-based illustrations included in this book. He beautifully captured student learning outside of schools and Individualized Education Plans (IEPs) (McCloskey, 2022). Loralie Baum and Matt Barnes, two of my dearest friends, have been an endless supply of encouragement, and I am eternally grateful to them. I'm indebted to the folks who assisted with the development of the reflection questions at the end of the four chapters that focus on parent narratives: Allison Smith, Ben Simson, Gigi Gigglberger, Jeremiah Henderson, Kristen Crawford, Dr. Liz Murray, Phyliss Harris, and Sherry Skipper-Spurgeon. My friends in California, New York, and in other places near and far, thank you for having a positive impact on my life.

My parents, Carolyn and William Vogel, thank you for your support and love. My sister Kathryn is the epitome of strength and guts, and is an amazing teacher in her own right. Amy and Gary Howerth, and the extended Campbell family, thank you for allowing me to join your close-knit circle. I'm proud to be part of a lineage of public school educators: my aunt, Regina Vogel, my nephew, David Aveta, and my cousins, Patricia DePinto and Richard DePinto. Thank you for supporting students and families. My husband Sean is the quantitative to my qualitative. He has been a source of joy and laughter and continues to do the heavy lifting of meal planning and prep while I read and research. Thank you for your patience with me. I can't guarantee it will get any easier.

Extreme gratitude to the Mechanics Library and Chess Room in San Francisco, California, for creating a quiet space of solitude that was instrumental in the development and organization of this book. Many a rainy Saturday and weekday evenings were spent holed up within the labyrinth of books with my notebook and computer.

Finally, to the parents who collaborated with me in this work: Thank you for entrusting me to share your stories. This is an important step in an emancipatory mind shift in special education that I will continue to champion.

I
ISSUES IN PARENTAL ENGAGEMENT

CHAPTER 1

Introduction

For many parents who have a child born with a disability, or who have a disability diagnosed in childhood, a good portion of what they expected or were given advice on before their child was born no longer applies. They cannot walk into a bookstore or a library, go to the parenting section and pick up a book at random with the expectation that their child will be described. These parents and families go through the arduous and lengthy process of having their child assessed for special education services, and if they qualify, an Individualized Education Plan (IEP) is developed.

Students who receive special education services have multidisciplinary teams charged with the development and implementation of the student's IEP. Multidisciplinary teams consist of the student's parent or legal guardian, a school administrator, a general education teacher, a special education teacher, a school psychologist, any school-based related service providers, and anyone whom the parents believe should participate. The IEP is a legal document that defines a student's eligibility for special education. It describes how a student's education is impacted by their disability, and outlines goals, accommodations, and services that should assist the student in accessing the curriculum. Parents are the most important members of the IEP team, but many encounter hurdles that decenter their knowledge, as well as their participation in meetings that involve their children (Larios & Zetlin, 2022; Pushor, 2012). Even though their participation in the process is mandated by law, families encounter obstacles that deny them access to information. Middle-class families, as well as families who have traditionally been granted entry to hegemonic structures, are better able to access resources and learn how to navigate the system, while families from traditionally marginalized, minoritized, and oppressed groups often struggle to navigate the system (McLeod, 2022; Trainor, 2010a; Trainor, 2010b). This book aims to investigate the experiences of culturally and linguistically diverse (CLD) families, as well as the empowerment that accompanies recognizing the community cultural wealth (CCW) of students and parents,[1] with the intention of utilizing a frame that is centered in both CCW and disability studies in education (DSE) to inform the practices of special education support teams. This is an extension of the work conducted to fulfill my doctoral dissertation (Vogel-Campbell, 2021) in the area of educational leadership for social justice.

Under the Individuals with Disabilities Education Act (IDEA), parents and families of students with special education services are guaranteed the right to meaningfully participate in their child's Individualized Education Plan (IEP) (Bateman, 2017; Weber, 2013). It is the responsibility of public school districts, county offices of education, and, in the state of California, the special education local planning areas (SELPAs) to engage parents in a meaningful manner, and to establish partnerships with them in order to effectively draft and implement an IEP for students. In order to provide a comprehensive understanding of the problem of practice, we will first discuss four key areas where inequities exist: readability of IEP documents, translation and linguistic needs, funding of specialized programs, and the cultural mismatch that often exists between school staff and the families they serve.

At every IEP meeting, schools are required to provide parents with a "Notice of Procedural Safeguards," which in the state of California is a nineteen-page document outlining the rights of parents and students with disabilities. The IDEA reauthorization of 2004 mandated that parents be offered a copy of this document at the time of their child's initial evaluation for special education, as well as at every IEP meeting. Culturally and linguistically diverse (CLD) families of students with disabilities are tasked with navigating the puzzling and convoluted system of special education in addition to the societal oppressions and injustices they encounter on a daily basis. Oftentimes, systemic barriers, as well as a lack of resources, cultural mismatch, and misunderstanding, prevent CLD families from participating meaningfully in their child's education.

Parents are often provided the "Notice of Procedural Safeguards" at the beginning of a meeting with little or no time to read or process the information within (Duffy-Sherr, 2021; Fitzgerald & Watkins, 2006). IEPs are complicated documents, composed of difficult academic language that is inaccessible to many parents. In 2003, the National Institute of Adult Literacy stated that nearly half of American adults struggled to read a

---

1. While I refer most frequently to parents, it is also essential to consider the other members of a student's family that may take on parenting roles: siblings, grandparents, aunts, uncles, and so forth. To this end, I will use "parents" and "family" interchangeably at times.

document in order to analyze and synthesize information (Kutner et al., 2006). Mandic et al. (2012) found that 94 percent of the procedural safeguards documents were written at a postsecondary reading level. The remaining 6 percent were written at a high school level. Slow progress has been made; Gray et al. (2019) stated that 11 percent of documents were at a high school comprehension level, with the remainder more complex. Parents are often receiving information about their children in a way that is filtered or confusing, and they are not involved in the manner in which the IDEA outlines. As a result, the IEP meeting is often a dehumanizing process that creates distrust and frustration with the educational system.

In addition to this, effective language interpretation presents itself as a barrier to the involvement of culturally and linguistically diverse families (Wolfe & Duran, 2013; Lo, 2012; Jung, 2011; Harry, 2008; Lo, 2008). For parents who are not fluent in English, schools are obligated to provide interpreters in their native language in order to facilitate their involvement in the discussion surrounding the development of IEPs. However, if an interpreter cannot be found, parents are habitually asked if the meeting can proceed without an interpreter. Sometimes another family member or the student themselves are tasked with interpreting the meeting for the parent or guardian. While school staff may view these alternatives as successful solutions, these substitutions often result in denying parents the opportunity to fully comprehend the meeting. For example, when the student is asked to translate, a parent may focus attention on their child's feelings and the possible stressors that go along with listening to trusted adults document their struggles and difficulties in school. In addition, teachers may edit their remarks or mask underlying areas of concern if their student is in the room. When a student or family member serves as the translator, the parent may find it difficult to focus upon what the school team is proposing. These practices from both teachers and administrators prevent some parents from having a complete grasp of the meeting (Bakken & Smith, 2011) and deny them the ability to make fully informed decisions about their child's education. Larios and Zetlin (2022) go so far as to say that "the families that relied on an interpreter appeared to be a burden to the school personnel" (p. 18).

In addition to the barriers presented by written communication of the IEP legal documents and access to oral communication during the IEP meetings, resources, both fiscal and tangible, are limited for programming in special education. To date, the federal government has not fully funded special education services. State and local governments are expected to make up the difference in educating a child who requires special education services (Griffith, 2015). As a result, many programs for students with disabilities have been underfunded since their inception.

Beyond the structural obstacles of written and oral communication and scarce resources, there often exists a cultural mismatch among educators and CLD families. Many teachers lack cultural understanding to work effectively with the CLD parents and families of students on their caseloads. Education professionals' perspectives are often rooted within a deficit mindset perspective of students' abilities (Lalvani, 2013). There is a need to understand how to move educators toward assets-based mindsets of students and families in order to enact asset pedagogies (Waitoller & Thorius, 2022). One way to work toward adjusting the mindsets of educators is by incorporating the practice of cultural humility, a critical means of evaluating power imbalances in working relationships in order to facilitate partnerships with others (Tervalon & Murray-Garcia, 1998). Originally studied and implemented in the field of medicine, there has been a movement to adapt cultural humility practices to the field of special education (Sauer & Rossetti, 2019). This research aims to contribute to changing the way that students and families are valued and centered in the special education process.

HISTORICAL BACKGROUND ON DISABILITY AND SPECIAL EDUCATION IN THE UNITED STATES

Since the colonization of the land that we know as the United States, there has been a marked stigma of the "other." The American ideals of independence, autonomy, and freedom clashed with the perceptions of those with disabilities, who were seen as deficient and dependent. Schweik (2009) describes "ugly laws" that were passed in many states and cities across the United States in the nineteenth and twentieth centuries. San Francisco, the city where I have resided the past fifteen years, passed such a law in 1867 that banned diseased and deformed persons who were deemed unsightly from any public space in the city. This attempt at removing persons with disabilities from the public eye perpetuated the notion that those with mental or physical impairments were not meant to be seen or heard.

Access to education for those with disabilities was heavily influenced by race, gender, and social status. As a result, most of those considered disabled were denied any formal education. Laurent Clerc and Thomas

Hopkins Gallaudet founded the American Asylum for the Deaf, the first disability-centered institution, in Hartford, Connecticut, in 1817. The Gallaudet family was also instrumental in the founding and recognition of the National Deaf-Mute College (later renamed Gallaudet University) in 1864.

Public schooling in the United States was not designed to meet the needs of a diverse range of learners. In fact, until recently, students with disabilities were often excluded from the system entirely. Nielsen (2012) states that "disability, as a concept, was used to justify legally established inequalities" (p. 50). Before the passing of PL 94-142, the Education for All Handicapped Children Act (EAHCA) in 1975, public schools were not obligated to provide education to children with disabilities. Only 20 percent of children identified with a disability attended public schools in 1970 (Yell et al., 2022). Furthermore, some states had laws that explicitly excluded children with specific disabilities from receiving an education at their local public schools, including students who were blind, deaf, emotionally disturbed, or who had cognitive impairments. The majority of these students were sent to specialized state schools or were institutionalized. Families were encouraged by doctors at these institutions to never mention these children in order to preserve the sanctity of marriages and for the sake of other children in their families.

The Elementary and Secondary Education Act (ESEA) of 1965 introduced the concept of federal aid to schools, but this did not include funding specifically for the education of students with disabilities. The ESEA was amended in 1970 to include the Education of the Handicapped Act (EHA), which earmarked funding for states to improve services for students with disabilities. It also created grants for colleges and universities to prepare teacher candidates to serve students with disabilities. Though this was an important step, the EHA did not grant any rights to students with disabilities.

The Education for All Handicapped Children Act of 1975, or EAHCA, changed things drastically. It stated public school districts were obligated to assess students suspected of a disability, and guaranteed that special education services were available to students who needed them, in the form of an IEP. The law also required school districts to provide a free, appropriate, public education (FAPE) in the least restrictive environment (LRE), with maximum opportunities to interact with their peers who did not have disabilities. Assigning students with disabilities to separate schools was only deemed appropriate when goals and services established to make meaningful educational progress could not be achieved in the general education classroom or school site. Finally, the law developed an oversight process for special education services to ensure consistency and accountability to the students they served. EAHCA provided federal funds for programs for students with disabilities (Spaulding & Pratt, 2015). All states had complied with all of the required provisions of EACHA by 1985 (Yell et al., 2022). In 1990, EAHCA was reauthorized and renamed the Individuals with Disabilities Education Act (IDEA). This reauthorization went deeper into defining both student and parent rights and focused on inclusive services and practices for students with disabilities, as well as the development of procedural safeguards that outline the protections and rights of students and parents with an IEP (Katsiyannis et al., 2001). IDEA has been reauthorized and amended three times, in 1997, 2004, and 2015. The 2015 amendment was part of the Every Student Succeeds Act (ESSA), which reauthorized the Elementary and Secondary Education Act (ESEA). Under this version of the law, students with disabilities are held to standards equivalent to their typically developing peers, and parameters for statewide testing for students with disabilities are reworded and expanded to allow states to develop alternative assessments for students with significant cognitive delays. In addition, the law requires individual states to develop plans to address empirical studies that reveal that students with disabilities are more likely to be bullied than general education students.

CULTURALLY AND LINGUISTICALLY DIVERSE STUDENTS

There is no one agreed-upon definition for the term *culturally and linguistically diverse*. Hammond (2014) uses *students of color* and *culturally and linguistically diverse students* interchangeably in her work. For the purpose of this research, culturally and linguistically diverse students include any students whose first or dominant languages are not English, as well as students who come from minoritized and oppressed communities (Harris et al., 2019). Since its inception, the United States has made a concerted effort to maintain English as the dominant language. Following is a brief discussion of the ways in which systemic White supremacy has upheld the oppressive mechanisms that have denied these students equitable opportunities to a public education.

In 1968, Title VII of the ESEA (Elementary and Secondary Education Act) established a policy for students with limited English proficiency (LEP), however, this was an unfunded mandate and was generally not enforceable. With the 1974 ruling in *Lau v. Nichols* came an increased awareness of the needs of English language learners, as well as a renewed Bilingual Education Act (BEA) and substantial funding (Gándara et al., 2010). The Office of Civil Rights (OCR) provided some oversight of the new mandates, especially in larger, urban school districts (Gándara et al., 2004). However, these funds were cut again toward the end of the 1970s, and the decades that followed saw increased calls for monolingual education.

The voters in the state of California passed two significant propositions in the 1990s that further endangered educational opportunities for CLD students. First, Proposition 187 in 1994 barred undocumented immigrants from receiving public services, including education (Martin, 1995). Then, Proposition 227 in 1998 decreed that instruction in California public schools was strictly English only. This essentially eliminated bilingual education in California (Gándara et al., 2000). Proposition 227 was repealed in 2016 with the passage of Proposition 58. This law grants school districts the ability to establish English immersion programs for English language learners (ELL) as well as English only (EO) students (Taylor & Udang, 2016). Proposition 58 was the first law in California mandating that parents of ELLs be directly involved in stakeholder engagement activities during the local control accountability plan (LCAP) process. Parents of ELLs continue to maintain a presence in advisory committees, specifically with the English Learner Advisory Committee (ELAC) at the school site level and the District English Learner Advisory Council (DELAC) at the district level.

RESEARCH PURPOSE AND SIGNIFICANCE

The concept of accessibility for culturally and linguistically diverse families is often implemented through the narrow lens of legal compliance, specifically what districts and schools are obligated to provide, as opposed to one of equity, where ethical responsibility and social justice are motivating factors. There is a body of literature that identifies both the barriers that CLD families encounter in the special education process and the outcomes for students with IEPs who are inequitably served. What is not present are studies conducted by special education professionals in collaboration with the families they serve to identify procedural shifts needed to improve those outcomes.

There is a need to understand the experiences of CLD families of students with disabilities during the IEP process. Nicolarakis et al. (2022) state that such a lack of understanding contributes to the continued oppression and discrimination of those with disabilities. In addition to this, there is a need to study how an educator's understanding of students and families' community cultural wealth affects their interactions. Equally important is the necessity to create spaces for educators where they can have candid conversations about the systemic problems they encounter, as well as working collaboratively to problem-solve and instill an understanding of the community cultural wealth of their students, parents, and families.

I address this need through a participatory research project that involves engaging parents of culturally and linguistically diverse students with IEPs in dialogue to develop an understanding of their experiences with their child's education. With the purpose to better serve CLD students and families in mind, two overarching research questions will guide our work:

1. What are the experiences of CLD families navigating special education in a public school district?
2. How can an understanding of CLD families' experiences inform the practices of special education teams?

Based on my research questions, the following topic areas merit consideration.

- How do families describe
  - their child? What does their child like? What are their strengths?
  - their first discussion with education staff about their child's learning differences?
  - their initial contact with special education staff?
  - their understanding of the special education assessment process?
  - their ongoing communication with special education staff?
  - their understanding of the special education paperwork?
  - their expectations of the special education process?
  - the role they play in the designing and monitoring of their child's educational program?

- Based on parent narratives, how might we (special education teams) consider
    - the ways we can learn from parents about their child's assets, strengths, and interests?
    - the ways in which we can learn from initial conversations about a child's learning differences?
    - the ways in which we initially contact families?
    - the ways in which we share the assessment process?
    - the ways in which we model and support ongoing communication?
    - the ways in which we facilitate understanding of the special education paperwork?
    - the expectations that parents have about the special education process?
    - the roles that parents play in the designing and monitoring of their child's educational program?

The intent of this study is to center the narratives of parents in order to contribute to the conversation of structural and systemic change in special education. Gloria Ladson-Billings (2021; 1995a) so eloquently affirms this stance when she states, "We need to have an opportunity to explore alternate research paradigms that include the voices of parents and communities in non-exploitative ways" (p. 53).

POSITIONALITY

A common question that I have encountered many times throughout my career is "Did you find special education or did special education find you?" Working with students with disabilities is a career path that I actively chose, with significant influence from my personal experiences. During the same time that I completed my undergraduate work with a focus on cultural anthropology and urban studies, my nephew was diagnosed on the autism spectrum. Witnessing the struggles and successes that my brother and sister-in-law encountered through the early stages of his diagnosis and schooling drew my interest to pursue a master's degree and credentials in special education. I was, and continue to be, motivated to disrupt institutions so that the barriers my family encountered upon entering the special education system are broken down.

Over my nearly two decades in the field of special education, I have worked in a variety of settings and schools. The first five years of my teaching career I was the lead teacher in a therapeutic day class (TDC or TSDC) at a nonpublic school (NPS). NPSs generally serve students who have been moved from class to class in a district in an attempt to serve them. After all else fails, these students are sent to nonpublic schools, often a thirty- to forty-five-minute bus ride from their homes. At the time, I had students in kindergarten through fifth grade in my one classroom, which was staffed with three behavioral technicians (BT) and one master's-level therapist.

Our school was part of a larger agency that supported students and families across Northern California. Part of our initial onboarding included restraint training, which was only to be used when a student was an imminent danger or threat to themselves or others. During this training, we learned the importance of teamwork, especially in order to prevent the student from being injured in the restraint, as well as the safety of colleagues. Although I was not comfortable with the idea of holding down a student, I understood it to be a part of my role in this setting.

Over the course of those five years, at two different schools, I was witness to and participated in practices that I now realize were harmful, unethical, and, according to laws that have since been passed in the state of California, now illegal. I have spent years trying to come to terms with my complicit actions. Evans-Santiago (2020) stresses that it is important for educators to be open, honest, and vulnerable in reflecting on the "mistakes we have made," which is aptly the title of her volume. I cannot go back and undo those mistakes, but I can work toward repairing that harm and lead efforts to reduce harm in the future.

I am a White, cisgender, monolingual, upper-middle-class woman. Although I live with clinical depression and generalized anxiety, I do not identify as a disabled person. I serve students and families from a variety of backgrounds, whose cultural experiences differ from what I experienced during my developmental years. I attempt to live through an antiracist framework, which is counter to what I was exposed to growing up. I am continuously learning to understand how my implicit biases impact the work and interactions I have with colleagues and families. I also carry on the process of unpacking what it means to be a White educator working within an oppressive system but also working against that system in order to bring about a transformational shift that is sustaining to students, families, and communities. I consider myself an "insider-outsider" (Dwyer

& Buckle, 2009) practitioner-researcher. While some of my identity clearly positions me as an outsider, the time and commitment to the communities I have worked with for nearly twenty years cannot be discounted. There is nothing detached or dispassionate about my perspective of the students and families I work with, the initial definition of outsider research (Merton, 1972).

> Disability Studies in Education (DSE) provides a different paradigm in which families are viewed as partners in the collaborative process of designing holistic support systems that recognize the complexities and humanity of individuals with disabilities and their families. (Sauer & Rossetti, 2019, p. 10)

Likewise, in conducting a participatory study, I decenter myself as the sole source of knowledge and through emancipatory praxis (Anderson et al., 2007) aim to bring the voices and knowledge of peoples not counted in traditional research to light. New meaning is made through dialogue between community and among individuals.

CHAPTER 2

Literature Review

In this chapter, I will explore the following topics: parental engagement of culturally and linguistically diverse (CLD) families, compliance, communication and collaboration, perspectives and experiences of CLD families, culturally sustaining pedagogy (CSP), and cultural humility. Each of these topics aid the development of a deeper understanding of the problem of practice presented in the first chapter. I will then describe the gap in the existing research and how the research and findings presented in this book both add to and create the intersectional wealth of knowledge necessary to serve students identified with disabilities, as well as their families.

PARENTAL ENGAGEMENT OF CLD FAMILIES

While the literature on parental engagement is extensive, the majority of existing research does not take into account the multiple identities and oppressions that affect how culturally and linguistically diverse families are engaged and involved with school-based teams (Lasky & Karge, 2011). It is also important to note the difference between "parental involvement" and "parental engagement," as described by Fenton et al. (2017). The researchers quote Reynolds (2010) who states, "The term 'Involvement' used in this work refers to school-sanctioned, school-authored activities in which parents participate. The term 'Engagement' is conceptualized as encompassing those activities parents structure for themselves and their self-directed relational interactions with school officials" (p. 144).

In other words, to *involve* parents is often defined as including them into predetermined procedures under the control of the school. To *engage* parents is to empower creation of spaces where parents lead themselves. Gallo (2017) pushes us further to insist that engagement of parents and families *must* be authentic and humanizing. However, there are limited instances of authentic parent engagement in the literature, and even parent involvement is inconsistently demonstrated.

Based on their study of eight monolingual and bilingual Spanish- and English-speaking families of elementary school students with IEPs in a California school district, Larios and Zetlin (2022; 2012) determined that CLD parents are disenfranchised throughout the IEP meeting. For instance, Larios and Zetlin state, "Parents may feel muted if they are unfamiliar with the system of education" (2012, p. 283). CLD parents may not feel it is their place to disagree with education professionals, and may go out of their way to avoid conflict with teachers and other education staff. This may lead to feeling isolated, powerless, and alienated from the special education process (Hess et al., 2006).

Many parents do not explicitly choose to distance themselves from the IEP process; they have either been excluded or made to feel unwelcome. Larios and Zetlin (2012) state that

> when parents *choose* to exclude themselves from the IEP process or involvement with their child's school, the perception is that minority parents place little to no value on their child's academics and success when in fact it may be due to a growing mistrust. (p. 282; my emphasis)

Similarly, Jung (2011) asks parents to change and adapt but does not place the same onus on school professionals. He does challenge educators to examine their biases and ethnocentric values, but this is worded as a suggestion as opposed to a directive. He states that it is necessary for "immigrant parents to be more open to a variety of sources related to their child's educational issues by acquiring problem-solving attitudes and developing effective communicative competence" (p. 24). By focusing on the cultural otherness of families, Jung ignores the systemic problem of excluding those othered.

In their analysis of the current body of research, Gonzales and Gabel (2017) found that language was one of the most significant barriers to parent engagement in the IEP process. Parents who speak a language other than English were often viewed as deficient in their investment of time, money, and resources toward their child's education. In addition to this, the authors asserted that parental engagement that takes place at home and outside the school building often goes unrecognized by school staff. Murray (2017) laments that schools are missing out on the opportunity to learn from parent insight and the richness of parents' experiences.

Lo (2008) found that IEP meetings were scheduled at inconvenient times for parents that resulted in lost wages from work due to time off.

Some meetings were held without interpreters present; parents nodded their heads in acknowledgment of staff members speaking, but this was misinterpreted as consent. The facilitator continued the meeting despite this and physically gestured for the parent to sign in consent to an evaluation that they could not understand, nor was an explanation given in their home language. On paper, this IEP meeting would be viewed as compliant, but procedurally, there are major issues related to the parent's lack of understanding.

Some districts have a Special Education District Advisory Council (SEDAC), which is facilitated by district staff, but parent-managed groups are not as abundant. Community-based organizations (CBOs) often serve as an intermediary, as evidenced by Nava and Lara (2016) and Mueller et al. (2009). These studies explored the power that parents attain when they are part of parent-led groups. Nava and Lara (2016) investigated the impact of parent workshops and retreats within migratory communities in California's Central Valley. With the development of these partnerships, parents became advocates for their children and developed the self-advocacy skills in order to engage in authentic conversations with educators that move beyond compliance with paperwork. Yell et al. (2022) have named this "better practices" (p. 2). Along the same vein, Mueller et al. (2009) interviewed eight monolingual Spanish mothers of students ranging in ages from four to sixteen. The mothers reported having a deeper understanding of the special education process and felt support from their cohort members who shared their experiences. The parent support group also helped the mothers develop more cohesiveness within their own families because of the emotional support they received from the other members of the group. Like the families in Nava's study, due to their increased knowledge of the process, IEP team members were able to interact on a personal level, and trust was developed and strengthened. Harry and Ocasio-Stoutenburg (2020) provide an in-depth investigation of parent advocacy in their work, and how identity intersectionality impacts families differently. Their intention is to co-construct new meaning, definition, and avenues of advocacy that are accessible for families.

COMPLIANCE

Under the direction of mandates of the Individuals with Disabilities Education Act (IDEA), state education agencies (SEAs) and local education agencies (LEAs) are presented with an overwhelming burden to serve students who are identified as having a disability. Compounding this already gargantuan task is that the federal government has never fully funded its share of IDEA. As the IEP is the backbone of IDEA (Yell et al., 2022; Wolfe & Duran, 2013), this presents educators and school administrators at every level with the issue of achieving 100 percent compliance while navigating a system with built-in barriers to achieve this expectation (Voulgarides, 2018). In many ways, this changes what *compliance* looks like in the special education process. There is the ideal that may be documented on paper and the reality of day-to-day operations (Harry & Klingner, 2014; Harry, 2008). The difference between the ideal and the reality is greatly impacted by the degree of authentic parental input.

In their work on disproportionate referrals for non-White students in special education, Harry and Klingner (2014) point out that many self-contained special day classes (SDCs) are enrolled over prescribed or mandated size limits. This, in turn, deprives those students, many of whom are from culturally and linguistically diverse families, of proper services. An interviewed teacher stated that her untenable class size prevents her from making deep connections with her students, with an implication that her unsustainable caseload further prevents her from developing reciprocal relationships with families. Voulgarides (2018) found that many schools allot only one class period for IEPs in order to work around teachers' preparation periods and reduce the number of substitutes needed. This disenfranchises families by limiting their time and participation, and reducing their access to IEP team members to answer questions.

In addition to issues with compliance, there are also barriers that arise because of compliance. These issues and barriers are disproportionately impactful on culturally and linguistically diverse families. Voulgarides (2018) and Wolfe and Duran (2013) find that many school districts will "check off" that parents participated in their child's IEP meetings based on their attendance instead of their engagement in dialogue. They found that silence was often accepted as consent. Wolfe and Duran (2013) found that educators overwhelmingly dominated conversations during the IEP meeting and did not ask parents if they had any questions or concerns after each section was reviewed. The opportunity for meaningful input related to parents' questions and concerns was limited and undermined through the push for compliance. These researchers also stressed that IEP meetings were scheduled with little flexibility to include items not on the school-created agenda.

In addition to exposing exclusionary practices occurring within IEP meetings, Voulgarides (2018) examined the time spent on staff professional development that focused on compliance with paperwork instead of developing educators' knowledge of curriculum and culturally sustaining best practices to work directly with students and families. Voulgarides found that teachers would be granted release days to fix paperwork but were often denied professional development opportunities for instructional best practices. A district administrator stated that this was in order to "keep the state off our backs" (p. 20). One professional development session in particular lasted almost two hours, where an administrator instructed educators what documents needed to be printed with particular colored paper. A teacher in attendance stated that these meetings were mainly focused on preventing lawsuits.

LITIGATION

When conflicts arise in the IEP process, there is a legal process used to resolve disputes. Either party, parent or district, may file for mediation, where a neutral mediator comes in to work with both sides toward compromise. If this mediation process does not result in an agreement, the family may choose to file a complaint with the Office of Civil Rights (OCR) or the California Department of Education (CDE). Additionally, either party may file for due process, which is a more formalized way to resolve disagreements. Due process is structured like a courtroom trial, with evidence produced by both sides and with witnesses called before an impartial hearing officer (IHO), who serves a judge. In a study conducted by Mueller and Carranza (2011), 85 percent of the 575 due process cases reviewed from forty-one states, including California, during the years 2005 and 2006 were initiated by the parents, but only 41 percent of the cases were ruled in favor of the parents. The low proportion of rulings that support the parents' position regarding student support is an indicator that even after an issue is resolved in the eyes of the law, families may see this as an incomplete resolution for the child. In addition to this, Voulgarides (2018) emphasized that "the legal mechanisms that give parents the right to due process through IDEA are written in complicated language, require mastery of English, and are difficult to leverage without legal counsel" (p. 68). Another important factor to consider is that advocates and attorneys are only financially attainable for a select group of families. Pro bono or low-cost advocacy and legal aid services are an option for families without the financial means to fund full-priced attorney services, but the availability of legal representation is limited by staff caseload limits (Burke & Goldman, 2015). Families that have attained a level of social and cultural capital have access to more resources to advocate for their children, further emphasizing the discrepancy between families with privilege and those who have been denied admittance to hegemonic structures (Hyman et al., 2011). Issues surrounding communication and collaboration—between staff, and between staff and CLD families—will be explored in the next section, further illustrating how inequities disserve CLD students with disabilities.

COMMUNICATION AND COLLABORATION

While there is a significant body of research on collaboration between schools and families during the IEP process (Bacon & Causton-Theoharis, 2013; Edwards & DaFonte, 2012; McNaughton & Vostal, 2010; Olivos et al., 2010; Olivos, 2009; Harry, 2008), there is a lack of documented information on collaboration among school-based members of the IEP team. More et al. (2013) looked at how special education staff work with language interpreters for culturally and linguistically diverse (CLD) families. Interpreters do not have an in-depth knowledge of special education laws and procedures, but they are tasked with explaining the process to parents. To address this need, More and their colleagues recommend that time be set aside for case managers (the special education professional that is the point person for a student's education) and interpreters to collaborate.

In Lai and Vadeboncoeur (2013), Chinese Canadian mothers likened their relationship with school staff to that of a guest and a host. As the guest in the school setting, mothers felt their role was to be courteous and not make requests. These mothers stressed the importance of being a "good parent," of not causing trouble for fear that it would have repercussions on their child. Sauer and Rossetti (2019) also describe how mothers, at first, may be hesitant to disagree with education professionals but become advocates for their children after experiencing frustration for years. One mother stated that "it has taken me 18 of his 22 years to realize that the Special Education system is as disabled as my son Sachin is affected by his autism" (Sauer & Rossetti, 2019, p. 77). Some mothers feel lost and confused, even after many years of participation in

IEP meetings (Hughes et al., 2008). Mueller et al. (2009) investigated how participation in a parent-to-parent support group changed the perspective of Latina mothers of students with disabilities. While the mothers initially felt satisfied with their students' progress, after speaking with each other and learning more about the processes involved in special education, they began to see how their roles had been minimized and sought assistance (from professionals they had met during their parent support groups) to advocate for their children.

Ishimaru (2020) describes how educators often "listen to respond" when speaking with parents in order to compartmentalize parental concerns into preconceived assumptions instead of utilizing active listening and challenging their own beliefs. She also questions the practice of "cultural brokering," which is used to create a bridge between majority White educators and families from traditionally marginalized backgrounds. Ishimaru challenges that the culture being brokered is actually that of the families, and that systemically this cultural brokering does little to aid families in the process of navigating systems. On the other hand, Sauer and Rossetti (2019) illustrated the power of cultural brokering, especially with parents from immigrant communities, when the "brokers" served as advocates and counsel for parents encountering this experience for the first time. To this end, teachers self-reported that they were more communicative and open with parents who had prior knowledge and experience with the special education process (Lalvani, 2012). While a teacher's definition of what constitutes prior knowledge may be defined by a parent's ability to utilize and interact with special education jargon, access to the knowledge was clearly divided by class and economic status lines.

STAFF DEVELOPMENT

Traditional pedagogical methods do not take into account the multisensory approach to learning that students may benefit from, especially students who have been identified with a disability. In addition to this, as mentioned previously during this review of the literature, the emphasis on compliance often silences the voices and perspectives of parents and families. Educators need adequate and extensive professional development (PD) to effectively work with students who receive special education services, as well as to facilitate communication with their families. Teachers must have an understanding of families' aspirations, as well as their strengths (Hagiwara & Shogren, 2018). The majority of existing professional learning research is focused on working with pre-service educators, but very little exists in the area of building an understanding of how to collaborate with families, let alone culturally and linguistically diverse families. Collier et al. (2015) investigated the importance of professional development for pre-service student teachers and found that providing educators with professional development on how to interact with parents and families before they stepped into the classroom has a positive impact on their relationships with the communities they serve. Similar studies need to be conducted with in-service educators and related service providers.

Equally important is that school administrators also need continued professional development (PD), in order to model for their staff effective ways of working with a wide range of learners and families. Designated PD times scheduled by school districts are often teacher-focused, and principals and other administrators are busy providing training to their own staff. According to Bakken and Smith (2011), the leader "plays an undisputed role in establishing a vision and setting the tone for school climate and working with CLD students with learning disabilities (LD) and their parents" (p. 35). Bakken and Smith further specify key responsibilities in an administrator's job that can have a positive effect on the overall school culture: an effective school improvement plan (SIP), recruiting and retaining staff, development of culturally proficient and responsive curriculum and resources, developing relationships with families and community partners, supporting ongoing professional learning communities (PLCs), and developing and sustaining effective programs for students who receive special education.

PERSPECTIVES AND EXPERIENCES OF CLD FAMILIES

Empirical research on the perspectives and experiences of parents and families of students identified with a disability is largely dominated by the experiences of mothers. Researchers engaging in critical analysis and discussion remain tied to traditional gendered norms and expectations of mothers and fathers. Studies that state they are focusing on parents tend to rely on mothers for the majority of their data (Lai & Vadeboncoeur, 2013; Lo, 2008; Hughes et al., 2002). In other words, "parents" often only means "mother" in investigations of family involvement. Few studies specifically focus on perspectives of fathers and male identified parental figures (Gallo, 2017; Mueller & Buckley, 2014a; 2014b). One of the exceptions in the body of research is Gallo (2017), whose work highlights the engagement and participation of Mexican immigrant fathers in their child's education. In *Mi Padre*, she stresses to educators the importance of reaching out to male parental figures in addition to mothers, and how this further strengthens the bonds between school and home.

Zetlin and Curic (2014) analyzed parents' satisfaction, or lack thereof, with the IEP process. A major theme that came out of the surveys with parents was that the IEP process felt depersonalized, provoking feelings of powerlessness and invisibility. Engaging with families and making them feel valued involves verbal and nonverbal cues. Making eye contact, greeting parents with a smile, offering a handshake, bow, or a welcoming wave can convey a sense of caring and empathy. In this study, many parents felt that educators did not take their feelings or thoughts into consideration. The IEP process brought out strong negative feelings and emotional angst. Some parents disliked IEP meetings so much that they drank to cope with anxiety the night before. Zetlin and Curic (2014) also found that IEP meetings are structured on asymmetrical relationships "when there is an imbalance of knowledge, power, and authority" (p. 379). When power imbalances exist, true partnership cannot be achieved.

A child's parent/guardian/advocate may not necessarily be their biological mother or father; at times, grandparents, older siblings, and other extended family members fulfill this role and these perspectives must be honored and accounted for. Familial capital (Yosso, 2005) is an important part of the lives of students in public schools. While there is some research that directly involves grandparents in providing their perceptions of their grandchildren's disabilities (Katz & Kessel, 2002; Schilmoeller & Baranowski, 1998; Gardner et al., 1994), these studies were conducted with participants exclusively from middle-class Caucasian samples.

Of most relevance to this study is the work of Sauer and Rossetti (2019), as they engage in dialogue with their participants to create strengths-based portraits of six families of children with disabilities. Siblings, aunts, and uncles all contribute to the research through first- and secondhand accounts of their journeys and experiences. Through poetry, Kimiya, the sister of a young woman with cerebral palsy, shares her sister's favorite things, and documents the struggle the entire family undertook when advocating for her care. She stresses the need for educators and related service providers to "consider how their tones and words influence the way families and their children regard themselves" (Sauer & Rossetti, 2019, p. 100) and recognize that each family and culture views disability through a different lens. Understanding one's positionality, power structures, and impact on the special education process may require educators to intentionally examine their use of verbal and nonverbal language with students, parents, and families.

CULTURAL HUMILITY

The disparity between the racial and cultural backgrounds of public school teachers and their students and families deepens the already existing power imbalance. The California School Dashboard (2023) reported that 78 percent of the approximately 5.9 million public school K–12 students identified as a race other than White; however, 2018–19 statistics (the most current numbers available) from CalEdFacts (2023) state that 61 percent of the approximately three hundred thousand K–12 public school teachers in California identified as White. Many school districts have engaged their staff in professional development focused on cultural competency. The issue with this is that as a concept, competency is seen as a benchmark to be achieved, with little follow-up after one is deemed "competent." The emphasis placed on competency and compliance is in many ways oppositional toward our goal of engagement. Instead, what is needed is cultural humility, which is defined as a means of lifelong self-evaluation and reflection to commit oneself toward eliminating power imbalances that exist between two or more parties, with the hope of developing positive outcomes (Foronda et al., 2016; Hook et al., 2013; Tervalon & Murray-Garcia, 1998).

Cultural humility as a practice originated in the field of medicine in the late 1990s (Tervalon & Murray-Garcia, 1998), and has only just begun to enter the field of special education (Sauer & Rossetti, 2019). In their seminal work on the topic, Tervalon and Murray-Garcia (1998) found that while patients from historically minoritized backgrounds asked for the same amount of information as White patients, they received less information, with fewer details, and were spoken to in a negative and patronizing manner. A practitioner of cultural humility would be aware of the history of interactions with doctors and patients of color, and intentionally communicate with the aim of easing anxiety, frustration, or distrust. In support of a cultural humility approach, Hook et al. (2013) found that clients who sought treatment from psychologists with high levels of cultural humility had more positive treatment results and reported a stronger working rapport with their clinician. This has major implications in the field of education and is a parallel to how parents report being addressed in IEP meetings. Similarly, Sauer and Rossetti (2019) advocate for cultural humility-based practices in schools in order to facilitate more meaningful relationships with students and families. Cultural humility is an essential aspect of pedagogies grounded in an understanding of the cultures of our students, which will be discussed next.

CULTURALLY SUSTAINING PEDAGOGY

Lifelong learning is a value that educators hope to instill in their students; however, teachers most often deliver instruction similar to how they were taught in school (Love, 2019). The pedagogy of public education is dominated by the perpetuation of a White, English, monolingual, ableist, classist, xenophobic, cisheteronormative narrative (Paris & Alim, 2017). Students of color, students whose first language is not English, students on the LGBTQIA+ spectrum, students identified with a disability, among others, are positioned as less-than and deficient in the classroom, which only increases the educational debt (Ladson-Billings, 2006) owed to students that have been dehumanized, oppressed, and minoritized. Scholars working within critical race theory (CRT) have developed and advocated for emancipatory pedagogy for decades. Two alternatives to the dominant narrative are culturally relevant pedagogy (CRP) (Ladson-Billings, 2021; 1995a; 1995b; 1992) and culturally sustaining pedagogy (CSP) (Paris & Alim, 2017; Paris, 2012). CRP and CSP are two examples of asset pedagogies (APs) (Waitoller & Thorius, 2022).

Culturally relevant pedagogy, as explained by Ladson-Billings, is a product of the classroom where all students experience academic success, where they develop and maintain cultural competence, and where they are given the space to challenge the status quo (2021; 1995a; 1995b). Ladson-Billings's (1992) coining of the term centered on eight teachers who successfully taught African American students. These educators utilized elements of students' culture to engage them in the learning process. Ladson-Billings stated that these practices should be part of sound teaching practices and expressed concern about why this behavior is not consistent across educational settings. Building off Ladson-Billings's culturally relevant pedagogy, as well as recognizing its limitations, Paris (2012) proposed that "culturally sustaining pedagogy" was the more appropriate term. He declared that to be "relevant" does not go far enough in ensuring that students' cultures are valued and validated in the classroom setting. With the addition of the verb *sustain*, he charged educators and students to take an active role in advocating for schools to "perpetuate and foster-to-sustain linguistic, literate, and cultural pluralism" (Paris, 2012, p. 93). Ladson-Billings (2014) supported this "remixing" of her thoughts to meet the needs of twenty-first-century students. By establishing connections between universal design for learning (UDL) and CSP, Waitoller and Thorius (2016) cross-pollinated pedagogies with the purpose of creating opportunities for students to participate in liberatory learning that honors and values their cultural selves. This, however, is one of only a few pieces of research that incorporated culturally sustaining pedagogy in the context of students who receive special education services. Gaps in the literature and current research further justify the need for additional work in the field. Waitoller and Thorius (2022) declare that educators and scholars of asset pedagogies must intentionally include disabled students in the research in order to be truly intersectional.

HOW THIS STUDY ADDRESSES THE GAP IN THE RESEARCH LITERATURE

Understanding the experiences of parents and families who navigate the special education process is an important piece of the conversation that is often neglected. With this in mind, a space is provided for chronicling what information currently exists, as well as naming gaps in the academic body of knowledge and research. Finally, the next section will explain how this research will address these gaps in order to better support culturally and linguistically diverse families of students with IEPs.

The review of the literature clearly illustrates a body of work that has contributed to our understanding of parent engagement, and parent experiences in the field of special education. However, most of the research focuses on the perspectives and experiences of majority White, middle- and upper-class families. The research highlighted in the literature review centered and honored the voices and perspectives of Black, Asian, and Latinx families; however, these different groups were studied in isolation, not in conjunction with one another. This is not representative of the school communities in which students, families, and educators hold membership. There is a gap in the research with multigeneous communities, and how the intersection of disability, race, class, and other factors contribute to parents' ability to access and participate in their child's education.

The research contained in this book brings the perspectives and voices of families from diverse backgrounds together, putting them in conversation with one another, and creating a collaborative space where their unique identities are honored, while their commonalities are recognized in order to strengthen the collective whole. By utilizing a participatory action research design, it is intended that families will play an operative role in this process. In reviewing research to prepare this review of the literature, there were no examples of this method of research conducted with culturally and linguistically diverse families. Therefore, this work will shift the conversation and thought to incorporate the capital that parents and families bring to the table. With this shift in mind, theories that frame the research—community cultural wealth and disability studies in education—will be further described in the following sections.

CHAPTER 3
Theoretical Frameworks

CROSS-POLLINATION OF FRAMEWORKS

I find it necessary to draw from both community cultural wealth and disability studies in education in order to satisfy the need for intersectionality that this research required. Waitoller and Thorius (2016) refer to this as cross-pollination, which

> enables existing elements of each framework to remain intact while considerations from one framework extend and enhance ways in which elements from the other have been defined and enacted. (p. 367)

THEORETICAL FRAMEWORK: COMMUNITY CULTURAL WEALTH

Yosso's (2005) community cultural wealth (CCW) can be defined as an assets-based framework that takes into account the experiential knowledge of communities of color that are often ignored or disregarded by systems of power based in a White, male, middle- to upper-class, heteronormative-dominated society. CCW comprises six different subsets of capital: aspirational capital, linguistic capital, familial capital, social capital, navigational capital, and resistant capital that interweave to create cultural wealth.

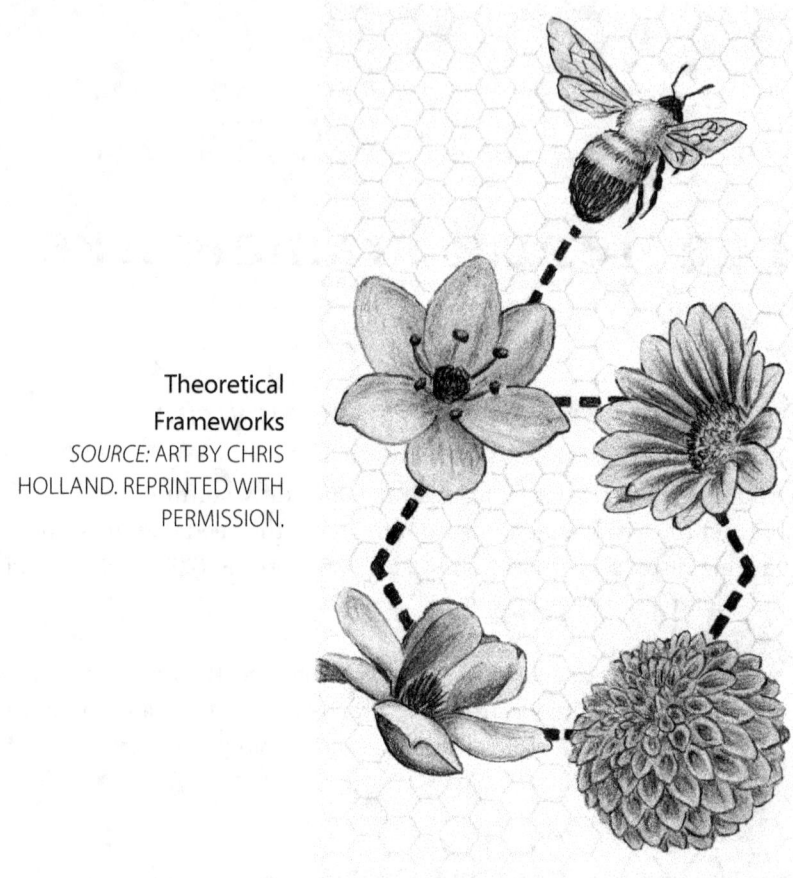

Theoretical Frameworks
SOURCE: ART BY CHRIS HOLLAND. REPRINTED WITH PERMISSION.

THE LINEAGE OF COMMUNITY CULTURAL WEALTH

The community cultural wealth framework is a branch of the LatCrit framework, which is itself derived from critical race theory (CRT). CRT was developed in the 1980s by Derrick Bell, Patricia Hill Collins, and Kimberlé Crenshaw, among others, who maintained that race and racism must be central to all conversations regarding inequity of power (Solórzano & Yosso, 2002). LatCrit arose from CRT as a response to the erasure of Latinx peoples in the conversation of race as it relates to a Black/White binary (Trucios-Haynes, 2000).

Tara Yosso, a professor of education at the University of California, Riverside, developed this framework in response to Pierre Bourdieu's (2011/1983) theory of social and cultural capital. Cultural capital can be defined as the resources that families can access as members of their communities and society. Educational institutions honor the knowledge of the upper and middle classes as valuable and productive to society at large, while the knowledge that deviates from this established norm is often disregarded. As a result, students and families from culturally and linguistically diverse backgrounds are often perceived as lacking in the knowledge, skills, and cultural capital needed to be equal participants in learning (Yosso, 2005). Therefore, through the theory of social and cultural capital, the school experience of students from traditionally marginalized communities is remediated, with lower expectations, in order to "correct" the assumed flaws these students possess.

Cultural capital, according to Bourdieu, posits that White, middle-class culture is the standard, while other cultures are inherently poor and inferior. Students of color are tasked with navigating a school environment where their skills and assets are ignored or viewed negatively. By introducing community cultural wealth, Yosso expands on Bourdieu's theory and is able to critically examine theories that have traditionally viewed persons of color as deficit-based. The community cultural wealth framework incorporates the tenets of CRT, specifically the centrality of experiential knowledge, to expand on Bourdieu's theory to incorporate the knowledge of communities of color. Yosso's (2005) aim is to "note the potential of community cultural wealth to transform the process of schooling" (p. 70). An examination of the six types of capital that make up the CCW framework follows.

ANATOMY OF THE COMMUNITY CULTURAL WEALTH FRAMEWORK

In order to provide a conceptual anatomy of the community cultural wealth framework, the following section provides definitions as well as research-based examples for each type of capital. Each of these types of capital—aspirational, familial, social, linguistic, resistant, and navigational—will be defined here with examples from the existing research. Fernández and Paredes Scribner (2018) state that "one form of capital does not usually exist independent of another; rather, multiple forms of capital are accessed at any given time" (p. 67). Thus, it is important to remember that even though each of the types of capital will be addressed individually, they rarely exist in silos. There is an intersectionality of capital and an exponential factor that operates to either increase or decrease power.

Aspirational Capital

Aspirational capital is the hopes and dreams of families for their children's futures. Parents place great emphasis on the importance of education as a mechanism for upward mobility and financial stability. According to Yosso (2005), aspirational capital "nurtures a culture of possibility" that envisions an end to past and current struggles within families and communities (p. 78). Therefore, obtaining an education beyond high school may provide children with more opportunities, happiness, and health than were afforded their parents and elders.

Familial Capital

Familial capital relates to the knowledge that is created, nurtured, and passed on through family, friends, and community. Yosso (2005) reminds us that in thinking about "family" it is important to move beyond the binary of blood relative/not related. Familial capital relates to kinship and collaboration, be it as a member of a "nuclear family," an extended family, or a community. Larotta and Yamamura's (2011) study emphasized how women participating in financial literacy projects first engaged with their husbands to develop a family budget, and then involved their children in a discussion about chores and allowance. Deepening connections with family greatly impacts bonds; this in turn grows the familial capital that bonds communities.

Social Capital

While familial capital is recognized as the knowledge created through groups and networks of people, social capital is the networks of people themselves, community resources, and the resources stemming from those networks of people. In their research, Fernández and Paredes Scribner (2018) look at how a Latino parent organization negotiated anti-immigrant sentiments and climate at an elementary school. The parents were able to raise their collective voice to express their concerns and disdain, something that would not have been attainable had they worked as individuals. Social capital was continuously exchanged and shared among the members of the group in the form of guest speakers, partnerships developed within the organization, and the activism that ensued. By working in community, social capital helps redefine who is considered a leader, and whose voices are valued in conversations surrounding leadership.

Linguistic Capital

Linguistic capital, as interpreted by DeNicolo et al. (2015), is the knowledge of language, social skills, and pragmatics gained through experiences in multiple languages and styles. For example, students who serve as translators for their parents in the community and when interacting with teachers have a sense of pride that their skills are a benefit to their families. The ability to communicate in two languages also serves as a bridge between a student's home culture and the dominant culture of the school system. By acting as a liaison between home and school, students are brokering language and demonstrating complex cognitive and language skills, which indicates forms of linguistic capital. While bilingualism and biliteracy are promoted at the secondary and high education levels, and are sought after skills in the workforce, knowing and speaking a second language is systematically discouraged in elementary schools. Even in situations where their home language is not valued in the classroom, students' knowledge is subversive to the narrative of the oppressor (Burciaga & Erbstein, 2013), which lends itself to resistant capital, as discussed next.

Resistant Capital

Resistant capital, according to Burciaga and Erbstein (2013), is "the ability to challenge inequity through subordination" (p. 27). This is counter to narratives of minoritized or oppressed persons who are often glorified as exceptional through their supposed resiliency, strength, and perseverance. Resistant capital is rooted in defiance and opposition to injustice. Chang et al. (2017) investigated resistant capital with Latinx students who were undocumented and demonstrated how they countered toxic and damaging narratives within the school climate. These students pushed back against the microaggressions they faced on a daily basis, reclaiming racist names and language directed toward them, and aligning as a group to challenge the oppressions that occurred on an everyday basis.

Navigational Capital

Navigational capital refers to being able to maneuver successfully through institutions that are not structured for the inclusion of marginalized members of society (Bejarano & Valverde, 2013). For persons of color, or persons from marginalized or oppressed groups, systems and institutions often actively work against their interests. To this end, navigational capital often works in collaboration with resistant capital as students traverse through their educational careers. As an illustration, in Bejarano and Valverde's (2013) work, students from migrant farmworker families entered the university system with little context regarding how to access resources and services. Through the College Assistance Migrant Program at New Mexico State University, these students "quickly create bonds through their shared immigrant, fieldwork, or educational experiences. This helps them navigate the university along with the assistance from staff who facilitate access to the university" (p. 27). This navigational support helps the students accrue and realize the cultural capital wealth they bring to the multiple assemblages to which they belong.

Application

Yosso's theoretical framework of community cultural wealth questions the dominant narrative of knowledge, specifically what knowledge is valued, and whose knowledge is disregarded. I view community cultural wealth as a guiding model through which we should structure our classrooms and frame our interactions and conversations with students and families. Conducting an action research project with a commitment to a community cultural wealth framework is aligned with the research focus on social justice and equity of voice.

THEORETICAL FRAMEWORK: DISABILITY STUDIES IN EDUCATION

The community cultural wealth of students identified with a disability, as well as their families, is often disregarded, because their status as "disabled" overshadows the strengths and assets they bring to school. To this end, I also aim to employ the framework of disability studies in education (DSE), in order to apply an intersectional lens to the problem of practice and research. DSE, is a framework that critically examines the concept and framing of disability within social and cultural contexts, that are increasingly expanding to include race, ethnicity, gender identity, orientation, and documented status (Annamma et al., 2022; Connor et al., 2016). Connor et al. (2008) define the four main tenets of the DSE framework as:

- Contextualize disability within political and social spheres.
- Privilege the interests, agendas, and voices of people labeled with disability/disabled people.
- Promote social justice, equitable and inclusive educational opportunities, and full and meaningful access to all aspects of society for people labeled with disability/disabled people.
- Assume competence and reject deficit models of disability.

In order to guide this discussion, I will utilize the five core concepts that Ferguson and Nusbaum (2012) identify as central to DSE. They state that the study of the disability must be social, foundational, interdisciplinary, participatory, and values based.

THE LINEAGE OF DISABILITY STUDIES IN EDUCATION

Although DSE as a framework is relatively new, its origins can be traced to coincide with the popularization of critical theory that questions dominant narratives. The DSE framework evolved from academic research in the fields of sociology and anthropology during the 1960s and 1970s, with a focus on the cultural experiences of those with disabilities. At the same time, the civil rights movement in the United States, as well as the disabled people's movement in the United Kingdom, provided persons identified with a disability the outlet to demand equality and rights in venues that had previously been closed to them (Baglieri et al., 2011). In 1980, Irving Zola began publishing the *Disability Studies Quarterly*, the first academic journal dedicated to the interdisciplinary study of disabilities (Ferguson & Nusbaum, 2012). Throughout the 1980s and 1990s, special educators began to examine the effects of schooling under the medical model of disability, which pathologized the person identified with a disability as deficient and aimed to remediate. DSE first started as a special interest group at the 1999 American Education Research Association conference. Over the past twenty years, the body of research focused on calling for advancements in education for students identified with disabilities to be equal to a student not identified with a disability, has grown. In the following section, five core concepts of the DSE framework will be outlined and framed in the context of the proposed study.

ANATOMY OF THE DISABILITY STUDIES IN EDUCATION FRAMEWORK

The study of disability must be social.

The pervasive view of disability is/was the *medical model*, which views disability as a problem that resides within an individual. The medical model has been the point of reference regarding disability in school (Baglieri & Knopf, 2004). School, therapy, and institutionalization seek to cure the problem. Self-organizing groups such as the Union of the Physically Impaired Against Segregation, which were inspired by Marxist theory, developed the social model of disability (Shakespeare, 2006). In contrast to the medical model, the *social model* views disability as the outcome of environmental, social, and attitudinal barriers. Persons and organizations working under the social model construct strive to remove barriers to foster full participation of people with disabilities. In other words, disability is a state of being that is defined by society, rather than something wrong or deficient with a particular individual. First-person accounts of those with a disability illustrate the complex identities of living in an ableist world. Liz Moore, in Wong (2020), describes how nondisabled persons advocating for cures for disabilities and ailments can be linked to the eugenics movement of the nineteenth and twentieth centuries. She states that "many in the Deaf and autistic communities do not want a cure and feel that those who advocate for a cure are advocating that they not exist anymore" (pp. 113–114). It is important to critically examine how our society and culture views disability, as well as persons perceived as having a disability. This leads to our next central concept of the DSE framework.

The study of disability must be foundational.

DSE scholars posit that disability is in itself a social construct, an additional "othering" to create a hierarchical system with a norm and different deviations from that point. According to Ferguson and Nussbaum (2012), it is essential to study disability because it will aid us in understanding human dissimilarities. Furthermore, Danforth (2006) suggests that

> the creation of the deficit notion of disability reduced a broad array of complicated social and educational issues involving race/ethnicity, social class, nationality, language, gender, and

schooling practices into a single problem target requiring professional treatment. (p. 79)

This deficit notion directly connects to one of the most prevalent issues in special education today: the overrepresentation and overidentification of students of color in special education programs, classification under specific categories, and the time they are excluded from the general education setting.

The study of disability must be interdisciplinary.

Disability must be studied in a variety of contexts: social, cultural, and historical, in addition to personal narratives and experiences. Along with the call for interdisciplinary study, the study of disability must be intersectional (Danforth, 2006; Baglieri et al., 2011). Crenshaw (1990) introduced the concept of intersectionality, which states that multiple identities affect the way a person is either valued or oppressed. Race, class, gender, sexuality, documented status, disability, and education are some of the factors to consider when utilizing an intersectional lens. Conversations and research that focus solely on one factor, or ignore the existence of multiple identities, are irresponsible (Annamma et al., 2013). Alice Wong's (2020) *Disability Visibility* is a collection of narratives that encapsulates the intersection of race, disability, gender, sexual orientation, religion, and documented status that illustrates the importance of recognizing the nebulous concept of identity and the impact that it has on individuals. When working with students and families, we must consider each element of their identity, and not focus solely on their disability. This is particularly pertinent to my research, and its connection to the community cultural wealth framework. In addition to this, Wong (2020), along with the contributors to the collection, exemplifies the importance of individuals who identify as disabled in constructing what disability is and means.

The study of disability must be participatory.

In addition to the call for participation for a multitude of disciplines, DSE scholars advocate for a central space for scholars who have an identified disability to contribute to the research (Connor et al., 2008). Furthermore, there is a call for research related to disability studies to be participatory. While participatory action research is not mandated, it is highly recommended, especially if the primary researcher does not identify as dis/abled. Danforth (2006) eloquently states that "it must be a scholarship transpiring *with* the disability community and disabled persons rather than a paternal regime operating *for* disabled persons" (p. 87).

With full transparency, I have been treated for clinical depression and anxiety disorder since my teenage years, and I am able to go about my daily life with minimal accommodations. While I do not identify as having a disability, this is a choice that others may disagree with or take a different stance based on their personal truth. My decision to undertake action research was not based on my own identity but as a movement toward equity.

The study of disability must be values based.

Perhaps this should be the first core concept in the list, but I chose to follow the order that Ferguson and Nusbaum (2012) provided. The only acceptable research related to persons identified with disabilities is that which frames the individuals in a positive manner, free from pathology or deficit. Much talk of inclusive education is framed within deficit thinking. Students who are in self-contained and restrictive settings are referred to as being ready or not ready for inclusion (Baglieri & Knopf, 2004). Framing sitting in a classroom with their peers as something needed to be attained is dehumanizing and another way in which students identified with disabilities are set on the school-to-prison pipeline. Exclusion is set as the norm for othered students; this applies to students identified with disabilities and students whose first language is not English, among others.

Application

Capper (2018) claims that critical disability education studies are minimally addressed in educational leadership for social justice conversations. Much like the binary of general education and special education, leadership and administration often exclude discussions of special education. At a district level, special education continues to work in a silo, and is rarely considered when discussions of equity arise. Even more problematic is the topic of inclusion; Slee and Allan (2001) state that "we are still citing inclusion as our goal; still waiting to include, yet speaking as if we are already inclusive" (p. 181). This applies to students identified as having a disability as well as their parents. Parents of students with

IEPs feel depersonalized and excluded from conversations around their child's education, and from their school community as a whole. It is only fitting to utilize the framework of disability studies in education in my work. I make use of the framework in my interactions with both staff and parents, including advocating for students with IEPs with assets-based language and for supports that do not exclude them from their entitled education. Conducting an action research project with a commitment to the DSE framework is aligned with the research focus on social justice and equity of voice.

There is a gap in the existing literature on the community cultural wealth of students and families in the special education system. At the same time, the DSE framework asks researchers to be both critical and intersectional. By combining the theories, it satisfies all of the elements needed to examine the issue at hand. The two frameworks guided the development of my review of the literature, in the development of my methods, and will guide my findings.

I center myself within the thinking of both frameworks so that I may communicate with staff and families with language that both recognizes and respects their multiple identities and realities. I will reflect on my process when I employ any exclusionary practices, either unintentionally or as an agent of an oppressive institution.

II

PARENT NARRATIVES

∙∙

The next four chapters will present a narrative portraiture of eleven parents whose students have differentiated learning needs. As previously stated, the main purpose of this book is to examine how culturally and linguistically diverse families experience the IEP process, and how educators might recognize and value the cultural wealth of their students and families. The overarching research question is: What are the experiences of culturally and linguistically diverse (CLD) families navigating special education in a public school district?

In order to gain an understanding of the journeys that each of the collaborators have experienced, the following related research questions are offered:

- How do families describe their child?
- What does their child like?
- What are their strengths?
- How do families describe their initial contact with special education staff?
- How do families describe their understanding of the special education assessment process?
- How do families describe their ongoing communication with special education staff?
- How do families describe their understanding of the special education paperwork?
- How do families describe the role they play in the designing and monitoring of their child's educational program?

The initial intention of the study was to identify the systemic and cultural barriers that inhibit the meaningful and comprehensive parental participation in the IEP process that is not only mandated by IDEA but is the moral and ethical obligation of educators to promote. In order to conduct this research, I obtained consent from the district to contact parents to recruit potential collaborators. All collaborators save one were purposefully selected based on my prior working relationship with them, or knowledge of their experience with special education. An eleventh parent was recommended by another collaborator. Upon receiving signed consent to collaborate, dialogues were scheduled via email and conducted over Zoom video conferencing due to the COVID-19 pandemic.

During each dialogue, the following prompts guided the conversation:

- Please tell me about your child.
  - What does your child like?
  - What are your child's strengths?

- Please tell me about your first discussion with a teacher about your child's learning differences.
- Please tell me about your first contact with special education.
- Please tell me about how your child was first assessed for special education services.
- Please tell me about your ongoing communication with special education staff.
- Please tell me about how you receive special education paperwork from your child's school.
- Please tell me how the special education paperwork is explained by your child's teachers and other staff.
- Please tell me about your expectations for your child's special education services.
- Please tell me about the role you play in the designing and monitoring of your child's educational program.

The flexibility of the semistructured empathy protocol allows for both participants in the dialogue to direct the flow of the conversation, and allows me to follow up with probing questions to clarify my understanding of parents' thoughts, feelings, and experiences. Some examples of probing questions include:

- How did that make you feel?
- Why did you use the word/phrase _____?

TABLE 4.1. Collaborator Demographic Information

Parent	Student	Age of Student	Grade	Primary Eligibility	School Setting	Languages at Home	Interpreter Used?
Emily	Ryan	10	5	SLD	RSP	English	No
Eiko and James	Nao	11	5	AUT	RSP	English/ Spanish / Japanese	No
Leticia	Isabel	14	9	SLD	RSP	English/ Spanish	Yes
Roger	Marcus/ Faith	11/13	5/7	SLD/ED	RSP/ SDC	English	No
Gloria and Tony	Jeremy	12	7	AUT	SDC	English/ Tagalog	Yes
Tomas	Isaiah	17	11	MD	SDC	Spanish	Yes
Lisa	Sam	9	4	ED	NPS	English	No
Vanessa	James	15	10	AUT	NPS	English/Italian	No
Judi	Betsey	10	5	ID	Home	English/ Mandarin	No
Aida	Hassan	11	6	AUT	Private	English/Urdu	No
Rachel	Emily	13	8	DNQ	Private	English	No

Note: Parent and student names are pseudonyms; other information is collaborator self-reported.

Using open-coded dialogue transcripts, I constructed a chronological narrative of each family's journey in special education. Utilizing grounded theory, I centered the words of the parents as headings for each section of the narrative and used quotes from parents to support the flow of their narratives. Table 4.1 provides a breakdown of parent-reported demographics.

A cross-case analysis indicates that, as a whole, the narratives illustrate the inherent tensions that exist between parents, schools, and districts, and all focus on the following themes: reliance on the status quo of special education process, (dis)regarding the parent experience, perseverance of parents in adverse situations, and the desire for assets-based thinking and collective problem-solving.

CHAPTER 4

Emily, Eiko and James, and Leticia

....

EMILY

Emily is a White woman with three children: a ten-year-old fourth-grade boy, an eleven-year-old fifth-grade boy, and a son born in late December 2020. At the time of the interview, Emily was still expecting her third child. Emily's fourth grader, Ryan, receives special education services under the eligibility category specific learning disability (SLD) and other health impairment (OHI). He currently receives support from a resource specialist, as well as speech therapy. Ryan receives occupational therapy (OT) from an outside provider, which is covered by Emily's husband's insurance.

"I don't think he has a bad bone in his body."

Emily and I are able to connect over Zoom the day after she starts her maternity leave from her job at a neighborhood grocery store. With two boys in elementary school and a third child on the way, Emily is extremely busy managing the multiple aspects of the household. Emily describes her son Ryan as extremely energetic and considerate of others. He enjoys some aspects of distance learning, especially when students are in small groups and "breakout rooms." Ryan wants to be the leader of group activities and likes learning, as reported by his mother and fourth-grade teacher. Emily reports that Ryan is sensory seeking, and moves around constantly, while doing his best to stay organized. Emily mentions that during his most recent IEP, which also served as his triennial reevaluation for special education services, his eligibility for special education changes, and that he receives additional services from a speech-language pathologist (SLP) as well as the

Emily, Eiko and James, and Leticia
Art by Chris Holland. Reprinted with permission.

resource specialist (RSP). Ryan receives OT through the family's private insurance but has not qualified for school-based services, despite Emily's multiple attempts over the years that have left her frustrated.

"We knew something was different; we just didn't know what."

Emily recalls that at around the age of three, she and her husband have some concerns about Ryan's development. She shares that the boy's pediatrician alludes to a possible medical diagnosis of autism. Ryan never receives an autism diagnosis, but begins to receive some speech and occupational therapy services through their insurance around that time. When Ryan enrolls in kindergarten, his teacher expresses concerns about his difficulty with focusing and listening. This conversation leads to an assessment and, within the legally mandated sixty-day timeline, Ryan qualifies for special education services under the category speech and language impairment (SLI). Initially, Ryan exhibits some echolalia, or the repetition of others' verbalizations. His vocabulary is also somewhat limited. With consistent speech services, Ryan's vocabulary grows, and the SLP asks to assess him again in other areas. His primary language issue at this time is using words in the proper context, and diversifying his conversational skills to incorporate nonpreferred topics. With a laugh, Emily shares that one of Ryan's fascinations is with kiwis, "so everything involved the kiwi" for a time.

"And I did a lot of fighting . . ."

As mentioned previously, Ryan has been receiving occupational therapy services through his parents' insurance since age three. At the beginning of our conversation, Emily says, "Occupational therapy is really hard for them to implement in schools." She describes how Ryan sits in his chair and falls onto the floor, and needs to move around during tasks. His private OT works with Ryan on core muscle strength and other sensory integration activities. Ryan's first-grade teacher utilizes an accommodation of preferential seating on the carpet, sitting Ryan near the back of the carpet so that he has extra room and can get up when he needs a movement break. Emily requests an occupational therapy assessment for Ryan but is denied. She feels that the district evaluation team "shut it down right off the bat."

Ryan's IEP team is aware that he receives private OT services, and Emily shares some resources with them so that they can be integrated into his daily schedule, but once again, she expresses frustration about the perceived ambivalence of the team. She states, "The Special Ed Department never really took that extra time, which as a parent was really frustrating, 'cause I was like, 'I know he needs this, but I also know that resources are slim too.'"

I ask Emily if the school team speaks or communicates with the private occupational therapist. Generally, IEP teams may ask a parent to sign a release of information (ROI) so that they can consult and collaborate with outside agencies and service providers. This is considered best practice and is expected of school-based teams in the district. I strongly encourage my teams to check in with providers that deliver services outside of the school setting, as this consistency frequently sees better results for the student across settings. Emily does not recall signing an ROI but states that the school team has not made an effort to reach out to the outside providers. It saddens me to think of the potential progress that can be made if the IEP team had worked in collaboration with Ryan's private service providers. I recommend that Emily request a release of information at her earliest convenience so that this collaboration may begin.

"You wanna do everything in your power to get them what they need."

Emily stresses the importance of finding time to create communication with school staff, because "they really don't have a lot of time for you." This is not stated in a condemning tone; rather, it is within the context of seeing how time strapped teachers and school staff are. Emily understands that she and her son benefit from her ability to communicate with school staff, and that parents who are not as involved can "slip under the radar."

Ryan has been working with the same school-based speech-language pathologist for the past several years. Emily recognizes the progress he has made, and believes that it is primarily due to the positive relationship that Ryan has with his SLP, as well as the SLP's understanding of Ryan's needs. The speech therapist frequently adjusts Ryan's goals as he makes progress and provides Emily with positive feedback and updates on a regular basis.

Unfortunately, the same positive history cannot be said in relation to Emily's experience with the RSP teachers that Ryan works with. Ryan has been receiving RSP services since the first grade, and during that time, he has had three different RSP teachers. Emily recounts her experiences with the two previous RSP teachers, neither of whom provide her with specifics on the work they are doing with Ryan, or with the progress reports that are legally mandated to be provided to parents on a quarterly basis. His first RSP teacher reads the IEP documents line by line in the meeting without explaining "the whats or hows," while the second tells Emily "not to worry about it" when she expresses concerns about her son's academic performance.

The paraeducator who is assigned to the resource specialist has been at the school site for many years, and is a consistent support for Ryan during his elementary schooling. She shares the tips and strategies that are effective for Ryan during his designated resource time, and has an extremely positive relationship with him. However, Emily realizes that the paraeducator is not "professionally trained in special ed services or anything like that," so her assistance and support can only go so far.

Prior to this school year, Emily does not receive communication from Ryan's RSP teacher at the beginning of the year introducing themselves. The new RSP teacher reaches out to her at the start of school this year; Emily believes this may be partially due to distance learning, as well as the fact that Ryan's triennial IEP is due early in the school year. As she continues to share the ways in which the new RSP teacher works with Ryan and reaches out to her, Emily changes her position and states, "This one feels like a really good match." She further explains that his new teacher "notices and attempts to help him with things that the others have never paid attention to." In addition to this, since the IEP, communication is consistent and ongoing, and the RSP teacher answers Emily's questions—on the same school day. I noticed how Emily seems to relax a bit talking about Ryan's current team and I'm relieved for the family that there is a sense of normalcy in this very abnormal school year.

"Thinking outside the box."

Even though Ryan is not receiving some of the resources that Emily feels he is entitled to, his school staff have been creative in finding ways to provide accommodations for his specific learning needs. Staff have bought items such as fidgets, yoga balls, and other sensory items that help Ryan regulate his body. Emily says that a weighted vest is suggested for Ryan at one point to provide him with proprioceptive input, but the district does not have one readily available for Ryan to use. I explain that this is generally the case, and that students who do not receive school-based occupational therapy services are less likely to have access to any of the stored items that a district may have, which is limited in scope. The staff at Ryan's school also provide him the opportunity to work in small groups more frequently, while still mainly participating in the general education classroom. Emily explains that he works best in heterogeneous learning groups, so that he is able to help and model for other students while some peers can do the same for him.

"Someone should have told her that."

Emily is aware of the privilege and capital that comes with being an English-speaking parent, as well as the role that implicit bias and institutional racism play in public education. Her son's school is a robustly diverse community, or "eclectic," as she refers to it, with Spanish, Portuguese, and Arabic being three of the other languages that Ryan's friends speak in their homes. She states, "I am so glad that we can live in a community where my children have friends with different traditions and holidays. It will help them become more understanding of peoples' differences." As an English-speaking parent, she has the knowledge to understand the paperwork provided to her at IEPs. Toward the end of our conversation, she shares that one of Ryan's friends who is also eligible for special education services had been transferred to a different school and program because there was no such program at his home school. The district did not offer transportation to the child's parent, a single mother of three children, two of which were remaining at their home school site. Emily alludes to the district withholding the transportation service to this parent deliberately because she did not know that it was something they were obligated to offer. Eventually, this mother was made aware of her son's right to transportation after chatting with other parents of students with IEPs. Emily refers to her "little support group" as a helpful resource but also acknowledges that she knows not every parent has access to peers in a similar situation. When I ask if she has heard of the district Special Education District Advisory Council (SEDAC), she states she has not. I provide her with the information for the next meeting and encourage her to attend via Zoom.

EIKO AND JAMES

James, a Latino man, and Eiko, a Japanese woman, are the parents of Nao, an eleven-year-old fifth-grade boy. Nao is eligible for special education services under the categories autism (AUT) and speech and language impairment (SLI). I have not been a part of Nao's IEP team; however, I am aware of the case because James is a school administrator in another district and his "insider knowledge" of the IEP process has resulted in the district's program specialist's attendance at every meeting to ensure that it's conducted properly. Nao currently receives speech and language services, specialized academic instruction (SAI) from the resource specialist (RSP), counseling, and assistive technology (AT) in the form of an iPad. Nao lives in a trilingual home: English, Spanish, and Japanese are spoken; however, English and Japanese are used most frequently.

"He has so many interests; he's all over the place."

James and Eiko describe Nao as a voracious reader who spends many of his weekends reading and visiting the library, including branches in neighboring towns. Nao has most recently been interested in various chili peppers and how they register on the Scoville scale. He loves video games, especially *Minecraft* and *Among Us*. Eiko tells me that her son loves history, and spends a considerable amount of time listening to podcasts on World

War II, nuclear history, and war. When Nao grows up, he wants to be a YouTuber, a comic book artist, or a video game developer.

"We saw signs when he was even in preschool."

When Nao enters school at age three, he has a difficult time lining up with his peers. His intolerance for waiting in line results in him hitting, biting, and scratching others when he becomes impatient. In transitional kindergarten (TK), Nao has a long-term substitute teacher, as the regular teacher is on an extended maternity leave. During a parent–teacher conference, James and Eiko bring up their concerns about Nao's impulsivity and aggression, and the substitute teacher suggests that they direct these issues to Nao's pediatrician. Eiko works as a paraprofessional in a special day class (SDC) for students with moderate to severe disabilities, specifically with students on the autism spectrum. While at work, she notices that her students' "little things," behaviors and nuances, are similar to Nao's actions and habits. However, when the regular TK teacher returns, their response to Nao's classroom behaviors is to say, "He will grow out of it." James feels that their concerns about Nao's social-emotional and behavioral development are ignored because Nao is meeting and exceeding academic expectations and milestones for students his age. Nao's parents' concerns are alleviated a bit when James's coworker, a special education teacher, observes Nao at home and at school and states she has no concerns. Thus, when Nao is in TK, his parents decide not to take their concerns to his pediatrician.

"Kindergarten is next-level."

Upon entering kindergarten, Nao's behavior increases in both severity and frequency. He begins to escape from the classroom and run to the playground when he gets too overwhelmed, to gain attention, or to avoid a nonpreferred activity. James reports that Nao has never left school grounds when he elopes, which might have resulted in disciplinary action per the school and district guidelines. At this point, Eiko and James bring Nao to Kaiser Permanente to see his pediatrician. The pediatrician refers Nao to the autism clinic where he is assessed and found to meet the medical criteria for a diagnosis of autism. A Kaiser caseworker helps them draft a letter to request a psychoeducational assessment, as well as a speech and language evaluation. After the school-based assessors complete their testing, an IEP is held to discuss the tests and determine Nao's eligibility for special education services. The school psychologist states that Nao does not qualify (DNQ) for an IEP at this time. James reflects on this determination:

> So we were disappointed because I thought, well, he could get some sort of service, but there was nothing. And we didn't really know a lot of stuff, and he was getting therapy at home, so we're like, "Okay, maybe that's okay." It was because he was doing academically fine, they told us.

James ruminates on how "maybe that's okay," because, just as in TK, Nao's academics are at and above grade level, and his behavior alone does not raise significant concerns from school staff. At this time, Nao receives in-home applied behavior analysis (ABA) therapy through his parents' insurance. For the remainder of Nao's kindergarten year, the school team will communicate regularly with the in-home clinician to support consistent behavior across home and school settings.

"Hey, wait a minute, something's not right here."

During Nao's first-grade year, James, a teacher in a neighboring district, enrolls in an administrative credentialing program and begins to learn more about special education laws and mandates. James states that as a general education classroom teacher he did not participate much in student IEPs, and mainly followed the instructions and lead of the site administrator and special education teacher. It is also during this time that Nao's first-grade teacher suggests that James and Eiko ask for Nao to be enrolled in a school-based social skills group. She notes that Nao is struggling with making and maintaining friendships, and that this group might provide him with discrete skills on how to engage his peers in meaningful ways. James and Eiko make a formal request and are denied on the grounds that this group is only available to students who receive direct service through their IEPs. As James recounts this, he visibly shakes his head in frustration, and Eiko shrugs her shoulders.

Eiko and James encounter another barrier during Nao's first-grade year, as they request their in-home board-certified behavior analyst (BCBA) to come and observe Nao in class. Their request is denied on the grounds that in-home services are not to be provided in school. Even after explaining that the intention is to merely observe Nao, the request is denied. James states that Nao's principal is trying to help as much as possible, but that the pushback is mainly coming from the district level.

Nao continues to exhibit difficulties with social interactions, and is again assessed for special education services in the second grade. The district conducts a psychoeducational assessment, as well as an assessment for speech and language services. This time Nao is found eligible for speech and language services, and is enrolled in special education as a student with a speech and language impairment. Eiko attributes this shift in eligibility to a change in staffing; at the beginning of Nao's second-grade year, a new school psychologist, as well as a new speech-language pathologist, are assigned to the school. James describes this as "turning over a new leaf," in that neither staff member had previously assessed their son, and thus they provide fresh perspectives on the support that students (such as Nao) may be able to receive.

"It's the two of us versus the nine of them sort of thing."

For Nao's third-grade year the family moves so James can take an assistant principal position and begin his administrative career. Nao's new district learns quickly of James's position, and convenes an IEP to review Nao's scores from the previous district's assessments. There are several additional IEP team members at this meeting, such as a program specialist and a special education coordinator. In addition to the speech and language services that his previous district was providing, Nao's new school offers RSP support in writing and time in the school's learning center, where Nao has access to a bilingual Spanish aide to support him with work from his general education dual immersion Spanish class. James, in a slightly frustrated tone, states,

> We fought for so long and now that I'm someone that they consider important, not only do they cave into every demand that we might make, they proactively push things for Nao and make things happen that I am sure they aren't doing for every kid. As much as I appreciate them looking out for my son, I know it's because they are scared or fearful of whatever leverage I may have if I get upset. Which, to be honest, isn't very much.

When James attains a position of leadership and privilege, it opens up services and possibilities for Nao that until then had been closed to the family. James questions this equity inconsistency. He wants staff to "look out for his son," but not out of fear of repercussions because he is a school administrator. James crafts a letter to Nao's new teachers at the beginning of each school year, letting them know that while he is a school administrator, he *was* a classroom teacher and understands to an extent the amount of work that goes into their role. He states, "I stress, 'Please don't be afraid to communicate with me,' and that I can help them if they are stuck."

During Nao's fourth-grade year, the school performs an assessment for occupational therapy, but he is not found to be eligible. However, Nao is found to be eligible for AT and has access to an iPad, as well as school-based counseling services.

"You should do it without being asked more than once."

James and Eiko report that communication has been inconsistent in their current school district. During Nao's third-grade year, he is in a class with two teachers: one veteran and one early service. Eiko shares that neither teacher is receptive to providing Nao with the accommodations he is entitled to as part of his IEP. "No, that's not gonna work, so I'm not gonna do it in my class" is the message that Eiko receives because of the teachers' ambivalence. Emails will often go unanswered, despite the teachers' understanding that James is a school administrator. As a result, James and Eiko call several IEP meetings throughout the year to get updates on how Nao is doing in class. Both parents report that fourth grade is like "night and day" and tell me that Nao's fourth-grade teacher is open to trying effective strategies, as well as brainstorming new plans in collaboration with the rest of the team.

"I have a Google Drive set just for IEPs."

James and Eiko describe themselves as extremely tech savvy, and request IEPs as PDFs so they can organize their files via cloud-based folders. Neither parent recalls receiving a draft of the IEP document prior to the actual meeting; however, they clarify that they have never explicitly requested this before the IEP. Eiko explains:

> It doesn't make a difference because we never sign anything at the meeting anyway. We will just, "Okay," and then will take it home,

and then we add things or we request more stuff afterward many times. They actually got so used to it that they actually said at the last meeting, "We know you're not gonna sign, take it to your home." And I said, "Of course."

This vignette demonstrates how both parents utilize the IEP meeting as a space to hear what the school-based professionals are proposing, sometimes for the first time, and then use time after the meeting to consider the offer of a free, appropriate, public education (FAPE) that the district makes. James tells me that he and his wife usually add a parent statement to the IEP if they feel the district notes do not accurately reflect the tone and outcomes of the meeting. While all parents are entitled to provide their comments in the form of an attachment that becomes part of the legal IEP document, in my experience most parents are not aware of this right. Eiko and James state that they always sign the annual IEP, but only after careful consideration and ensuring that specific language is reflected in the documents that meets their satisfaction. Out of curiosity, I ask James and Eiko if they have ever considered filing for due process against the district. Eiko responds, "Of course not, that will get us nowhere. We always want to work with the team and bringing in lawyers may close those opportunities." While this may be true to an extent, both parents have the navigational capital, as well as the resource of time, to negotiate and work through paperwork disputes with the school-based team themselves. Not all families have the same types of capital and privilege that James and Eiko have attained.

"They labeled us as high-maintenance or unique people."

James relays that Nao's school-based IEP team members are intimidated by his position as a site administrator in a neighboring district. At the same time, these professionals primarily speak and make eye contact with Eiko in IEP meetings, which James describes as an invisibilizing moment. He says, "There may not be many fathers in IEP meetings, so they may not be used to talking to us." He also makes the observation that the IEP team will refer to Eiko by her first name but address him with a "Mr." James believes this is mostly because the majority of Nao's team is female, so they feel more comfortable connecting with his wife on a more personal level. At the same time, he balks at the perpetuation of gender stereotypes in a relatively progressive-minded school district.

Eiko recalls a moment in an IEP during Nao's fourth-grade year during which she needed clarification for a technical word in an assessment. She turns to James and asks her husband in Japanese for an equivalent word. The principal becomes extremely agitated that James and Eiko are speaking in Japanese to each other, and asks to pause the meeting until a Japanese interpreter can be found to provide support. Neither James nor Eiko wants to pause the meeting and explain that the word in question is difficult for even a native English speaker to immediately comprehend. The principal reiterated her stance and the meeting was paused for several days so that a district interpreter could participate. James, visibly frustrated, relays that "they didn't trust me to speak truthfully to my wife and that was a breach of trust." Now, there is always a Japanese interpreter present at meetings, although since this incident there has not been a need for their services. James wonders how the money spent on this interpreter's time could be allocated elsewhere to programs and services for students.

As we end our conversation, James speaks longingly for the day that Nao can return to in-person learning. "It's time for him to be around other kids again," James states. Eiko is looking forward to IEP meetings in person, because face-to-face meetings "are so much more impactful than looking at someone on a screen," she explains. They are both optimistic for post-COVID schooling and working with Nao's school-based team.

LETICIA

Leticia is a Latina Spanish-speaking woman with a fourteen-year-old daughter, Isabel, who is eligible for special education services under the category specific learning disability (SLD). Isabel is a freshman at a local high school and is currently enrolled in co-taught math and English courses. When Isabel started middle school, Leticia began receiving support from Legal Aid, a pro bono or low-cost service for families with incomes below the poverty line. Leticia was concerned about how Isabel's services were being implemented, and the accommodations offered by the school district. The IEP team worked collaboratively to meet Isabel's unique learning needs as identified in her IEP. Leticia did not seek out support from Legal Aid during Isabel's eighth-grade year. Spanish is the primary language spoken in the home; Leticia participates in Isabel's IEP meetings with the support of a Spanish interpreter but is able to hold some portions of our dialogue in English.

"She's just a typical teenager with a kind heart."

Leticia describes Isabel as a social butterfly, who enjoys skateboarding, spending time with her friends, and making funny videos on TikTok with her younger sister. Isabel, once a quiet girl, likes to sing along to Dua Lipa, her favorite artist. Leticia's aspirations for Isabel are for her to attend college and then graduate school. Isabel talks about wanting to be a social worker, or working in a profession that helps people. Leticia thinks that this may be connected to her role as a Spanish family liaison in the elementary school district, "So maybe it's just wanting to be like me," she says with a wide smile.

"She'll catch up, she'll get it."

Isabel is a "young five" when she begins kindergarten, and Leticia has concerns about her daughter's ability to keep up with her peers right from the beginning. However, when she brings her concerns to Isabel's teachers, they do not share Leticia's worries. Instead, Isabel's teachers claim that Isabel is not significantly far behind and even caution Leticia about pushing her daughter too much. Leticia remembers that one teacher said, "In six months, they [students] just grab it [learning] and run." This narrative plays out in both kindergarten and first grade. By the time Isabel reaches second grade, her teacher admits that Isabel's learning is "taking a bit longer than normal" to fully develop, but again Leticia reports that the teacher downplayed her concerns about Isabel.

"Once I put it in writing, they were forced to."

Toward the end of second grade, after receiving advice from a family friend, Leticia requests that Isabel be assessed for speech and language services. At the meeting to review the results of the testing, the school team determines that Isabel does not qualify for speech or special education. Isabel continues to struggle during her third-grade year; in the middle of the year, the school team initiates a student success team (SST) meeting to develop an action plan to address Isabel's academic difficulties. After three SST meetings, the school team recommends a reassessment for special education services at the beginning of Isabel's fourth-grade year. In addition to reassessing her need for speech and language services, a full psychoeducational assessment is conducted to determine if Isabel would receive educational benefit from the resource specialist.

At Isabel's initial IEP meeting in the fourth grade, the school team determines that she qualifies for special education services under the eligibility category of SLD, due to a significant discrepancy in her verbal and nonverbal test results. Isabel also qualifies for special education under the secondary eligibility category of speech and language impairment (SLI), to address her auditory processing difficulties. Leticia is pleased with the results of this meeting, and describes how Isabel is able receive accommodations that make learning more accessible for her, such as having tests read aloud to her, extended time on assignments, and having a calculator to check her math work. Isabel receives resource specialist (RSP) support in the back of her classroom with a few other students for fourth and fifth grades. Leticia states that Isabel needs the most support with organization and generalizing math concepts.

At the end of fifth grade, Isabel participates in her transitional IEP meeting and is able to tell her new middle school team "what she wanted, what she felt she needed, and that was very helpful and impactful for her." For middle school, Isabel has a study skills class embedded into her schedule that continues to support her executive functioning and organizational skills, as well as a reading lab class after the regular school day ends that focuses on her comprehension and fluency skills. Leticia praises the middle school team for the work they do with her daughter and describes the three years Isabel spends in middle school as "some of the most successful of her life." However, toward the end of her eighth-grade year, Isabel is forced into distance learning due to the COVID-19 pandemic, like most school-aged children around the world. Amid the confusion surrounding the transition to distance learning, Isabel does not have a formal transitional IEP to high school, although Leticia is able to connect with her daughter's new case manager prior to the beginning of the 2020–21 school year. However, the lack of an IEP causes confusion about the services and accommodations that Isabel is entitled to according to her IEP.

"High school has been terrible so far."

Starting a new school in the middle of a global pandemic has been extremely difficult for Isabel, and Leticia expresses concern that her daughter is not receiving the support that she requires in order to succeed. Leticia finds herself taking on some of the responsibilities of Isabel's case manager and remarks that assisting Isabel with her readings has significantly improved her own understanding of written English.

Isabel has both text-to-speech and speech-to-text accommodations in her IEP, although Leticia states that these have not been implemented yet by Isabel's teachers. I quickly open up a blank Google Docs document and show her how to install the extension for text to speech and how to activate speech to text using the microphone on her computer. "How was it that easy and no one showed us? That could have been solved easily, it's too bad that was overlooked, but hey, it's a pandemic, you know?" Leticia states with a half laugh. She thanks me for this quick fix and states that Isabel will be extremely grateful that she can complete assignments in a timely manner.

"Hey, I need more time."

As she has yet to meet any of her teachers in person, Isabel struggles with trusting the new adults in her life. Leticia and I agree that it is extremely difficult to form relationships over virtual platforms. Despite this, Isabel has been able to self-advocate for her needs with her teachers when there has been either resistance or a misunderstanding about the accommodations she is entitled to. Leticia praises the work of Isabel's case manager, who has been instrumental in collaborating with teachers and supporting Isabel in the two co-taught classes she is enrolled in. Leticia explains that Isabel can access a "class within a class" breakout room where her case manager provides reteaching of concepts and small group support for Isabel and several other students with IEPs. Wednesdays are asynchronous learning days, when Isabel does not attend her regular classes but, instead, logs into a Zoom with small groups of students for additional support in any academic area. Leticia claims that this "makeup day" is a "life saver" for Isabel this school year, and that Isabel is earning As and Bs due to this help. She then clarifies her earlier statement and says, "Well, actually, high school hasn't been that terrible then."

"That courtesy call beforehand means a lot."

Leticia states that she has never had serious concerns with Isabel's IEP once it was put into place in the fourth grade. Throughout elementary and middle school, she receives a call from her daughter's case manager prior to the IEP to discuss any proposed changes. Leticia states that the meetings were often "just a formality," because she had opportunities to speak with all of Isabel's education providers before the IEP. In addition to this, she reports that drafts of the IEPs are always sent home in both English and Spanish for her to review beforehand. She stresses the importance of reviewing the paperwork before the IEP because "as a parent it's up to you to go over that and actually read it and look at some of that data."

As Isabel moves through the grades, the services that she receives through her IEP are reduced to reflect the progress she makes. Leticia states that, at first, school staff try to reallocate Isabel's special education minutes without her prior consent, to which she exclaims, "Whoa, wait a minute, you need to talk to me about this." After this first incident, Leticia relays that she is involved in every decision regarding her daughter's IEP, and that school staff make a concerted effort to provide her with the data to back up proposed changes they bring up at meetings.

I asked Leticia about how she came to be involved with Legal Aid, and why she retained legal counsel if she was satisfied with the implementation of Isabel's IEP. Leticia states that since Legal Aid was a free service it was a "no-brainer" to get that extra help. "It was an extra set of eyes making sure that everything was going correctly, and we never had to fight for anything more," she further clarifies. Leticia also states that at the end of Isabel's seventh-grade year, the Legal Aid attorney encourages her to sue the school district for reimbursement for a private school placement for Isabel. It is at this point that Leticia informs the attorney that her services are no longer needed. Leticia states, "I always wanted my daughter in public school, so that was a shocking thing for her to say. I was happy with how Isabel was doing, and at that point we no longer agreed." Legal Aid attempts to contact her at the beginning of every school year, but Leticia does not return their phone calls. "I said I was done," is how she ends this portion of our conversation.

"I question everybody."

Toward the end of our dialogue, Leticia stresses the importance of both parental and student involvement during the IEP. Leticia states that

> in order to get the services that you need for your kid, you need to be an active parent, and really know what they're doing and be hands-on with their education. And I think that gets missed by a lot of parents that might not have the flexibility to attend those calls or take time off work to be in the school to do that, so that's definitely a drawback. I don't think decisions should be made without the input of a student or a parent.

Leticia would like to see more resources available to parents so they can be educated about their rights. I ask her about her experience with the "Notice of Procedural Safeguards," a document that outlines parental rights that is available in over a dozen languages. Leticia states that she was provided the packet of information at Isabel's initial IEP, and the case manager offered to go through the document in detail with her prior to the meeting. Leticia expresses gratitude for that special education teacher's time and effort in helping her understand the nearly fifteen pages of heavy detailed information, much of it written "in lawyer talk." Despite the teacher's best efforts, Leticia recalls, "there were parts of it that the teacher wasn't so sure of. It's very long, so it could be super intimidating to a new parent." Since then, she has declined the "Notice of Procedural Safeguards" when it is offered to her and tells the case manager, "I'll take a copy when there is an update."

POSTDIALOGUE REFLECTION

Emily demonstrates a deep understanding of the privilege that she carries and how this directly impacts the services her son receives. By offering Ryan accommodations related to his fine motor and sensory needs, the school team indirectly validates his mother's concerns and this should be followed through with a formal assessment for school-based occupational therapy.

One may assume that the power and privilege that comes with first being a teacher and then a site administrator would clarify and expedite the process of seeking out and retaining special education services for a child. As evidenced by James and Eiko's story, even parents with insider knowledge and access struggle to navigate the system. The way that James experiences special education as a parent greatly impacts the way he interacts with parents of students that receive special education services at his own school site. Eiko, a special education professional in her own right, is considering going through the credentialing process to become a teacher.

Leticia's retention of a pro bono Legal Aid attorney so she had additional support at IEP meetings is a prime example of a parent utilizing their navigational capital in a situation that is often not designed with familial interests in mind. As a non-White, non-English speaking parent, Leticia is leveling the playing field by bringing this additional support person to her child's meetings.

Important Reminders That Arise out of These Parent Dialogues

- Make a concerted effort to introduce yourself to your student's caregivers at the beginning of the school year. Some schools, districts, and counties have implemented home visits for educators (Wright et al., 2018) and have seen increased levels of parent engagement. This may not be an option in your school. Reaching out via phone, email, or virtual meeting within the first week of school is essential to establishing a relationship with your families from the very start. Your site administrator may have wording they would like incorporated into any welcome message that reflects the mission and vision of the school. Be sure to get any correspondence translated into your students' home language.
- Become aware of local parent and caregiver support groups available in your city or county, as well as district-based groups. Some schools and districts may have a special education PTA (parent–teacher association), while others may have advisory groups that host guest speakers and are an outlet for parents to be in community with each other. Have this information at hand to pass along to your students' caregivers.
- In addition to sending home any necessary documentation prior to a student's IEP, connect with the parent to gain an understanding of their concerns so they can be adequately addressed during the meeting. Taking a cue from facilitation and mediation, ask caregivers what they hope to achieve during the meeting and what they aspire for their child. This usually alleviates anxiety prior to a meeting for parents and demonstrates that their child's school-based team is proactive in hearing their concerns.

Reflection Questions

- Discuss the benefits of having permission to speak with a student's outside providers. How can this inform your interactions with this student and their family?
- How can schools and districts support families with connecting them to community resources? How could this be done at your school or district?

- How can general education teachers take a more active role in the IEP process? What support do you think they need?
- What can we do as teachers/administrators to help make the IEP process clear and transparent for all families, regardless of race, ethnicity, privilege, and so on?
- What are the lessons learned from each of these three parent narratives? How are their experiences similar? How are they different? How did race, home language, and privilege affect their experience of the IEP process?

CHAPTER 5

Roger, Gloria and Tony, and Tomas

ROGER

Roger is a White man with two children who are eligible for special education services: his eleven-year-old son, Marcus, and his thirteen-year-old daughter, Faith. Roger and his husband, Jeff (who is also White), fostered and then adopted Marcus and Faith, who are Black, when the children were both under two years old. Marcus is a fifth grader who receives special education services under the categories specific learning disability (SLD) and speech and language impairment (SLI). He accesses the resource specialist once a day for a forty-five-minute period and has weekly speech, adaptive physical education, and occupational therapy services. Faith is a seventh grader who receives special education services under the categories emotional disturbance (ED) and other health impairment (OHI). She accesses one period of specialized academic instruction support per day.

I first met Roger two years ago when he and his husband moved to our district from a state on the East Coast. Implementing the services as outlined in those IEPs was a difficult task; school systems in other counties and states sometimes offer different services, or wording in the IEP is either too vague or too specific. I helped determine the appropriate placements in our district for both children and worked with Roger, who is himself an elementary educator, to make the transition as smooth as possible. English is the only language spoken in the home.

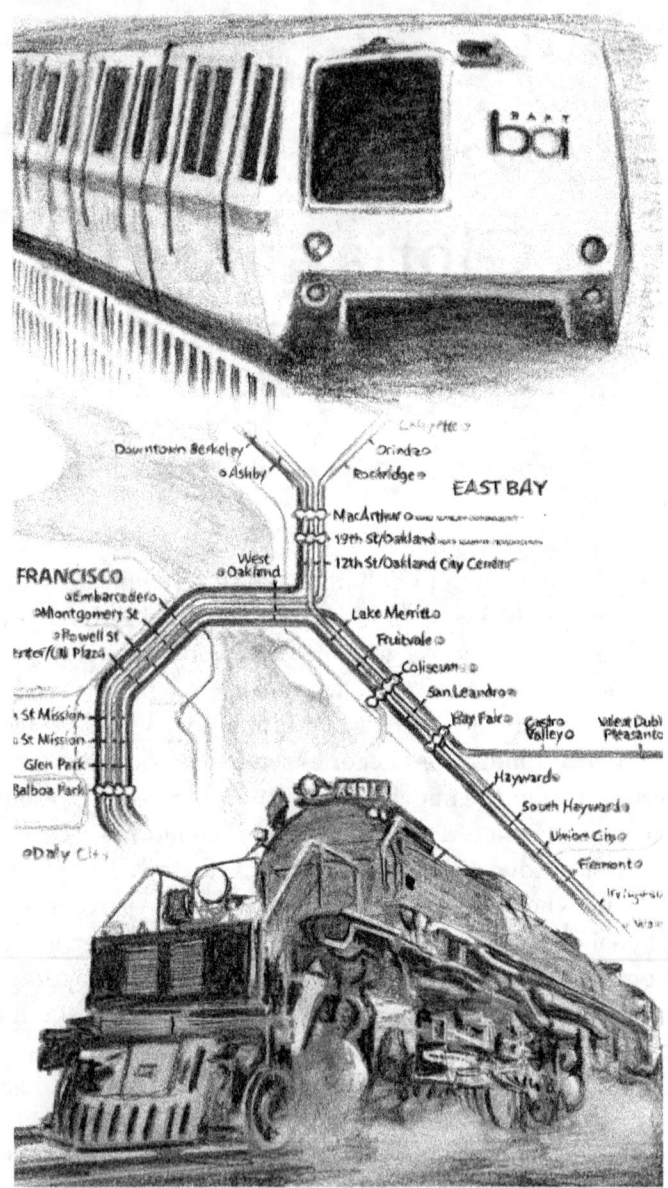

Roger, Gloria and Tony, and Tomas
Source: Art by Chris Holland. Reprinted with permission.

"It's different being a parent when you're working in the system."

I meet with Roger over Zoom shortly after the instructional school day ends, after our contractual working hours. Like most teachers, he has taught from home since the middle of March, all the while continuing to co-parent his two children, Marcus and Faith. Roger is extremely easygoing, and our conversation is peppered with laughter. He is one of the first parents that I envision collaborating with on this journey because of his straightforward communication skills. I am also eager to hear more about his experiences as a White parent of Black adopted children, a parent who is also an educator, as well as a parent in a same-sex marriage. The majority of our conversation focuses on Roger's seventh grader, Faith, since our working relationship is mainly based on implementing her IEP at the middle school level; however, he is comprehensive in his answers about both of his children.

"She just came fighting into this world."

Roger and Jeff foster to adopt both of their children when they are infants: Faith at six months of age and her nonbiological brother, Marcus, at ten months of age. Faith is approximately eighteen months older than her brother. Both children were exposed to narcotics while in utero and are entitled to early intervention (EI) services because of their developmental histories. Roger and Jeff enroll Faith in kindergarten in the urban public school district where they live at the time. During her kindergarten year, Roger requests assessment for Faith to determine special education eligibility but is denied on the grounds that she has not been in school long enough to determine eligibility for special education services. However, he states that the district is obligated to complete the assessment because they miss the mandated timelines in communicating with him and his husband. By the time the assessment is due to begin, the family is in the process of moving to a state on the Eastern Seaboard. With a bit of exasperation, Roger recalls how the one year in that school district is a "year of chasing down people," and how he is so tired that he just says, "Forget it," in regards to assessing his daughter until they move.

"We wanted a good public school education."

When it is time to move, Roger recounts that he and Jeff consciously select a particular town that is part of a larger metropolitan area because of the quality of the public schools, as well as the diversity of the student population. The school that the children enroll in for pre-K and first grade, respectively, is, according to Roger, about 15 percent Black. Marcus's and Faith's fathers value a racially and ethnically diverse school setting for their children, with Black representation being a main driving force behind their decision. In addition to students from the local community, a busing initiative is also in place to further desegregate schools. Overall, the town they move to is more affluent than their previous community in the Bay Area, and Roger requests assessment for special education services upon enrolling his children. Unlike his encounter with his previous district, the new school agrees to test Faith and Marcus for eligibility without question. Roger believes this is due to the higher-per-pupil spending, which results in more services and qualified staff. I later investigate, and find out that the district on the East Coast spends approximately $4,000 more per pupil than their first Bay Area district, as well as the one in which the children are currently enrolled (National Center for Education Statistics, 2020).

Both children qualify for special education services and are given what Roger describes as a "full IEP," with occupational therapy (OT), speech and language services with a speech language pathologist (SLP), adaptive physical education (APE), and other supports, as needed. Marcus has a "seamless" transition from pre-K to kindergarten. Roger and Jeff receive a great deal of support and feedback from Marcus's IEP team. Faith, on the other hand, continues to struggle, not just with her academics, but also her identity as a young Black girl with two White fathers, as well as finding her place in her school environment.

"Everything was coming to a head."

Faith begins receiving reading intervention services that are delivered in a pullout manner, to address difficulties with reading that Roger believes are connected to dyslexia. When she is not making adequate progress on her goals during her second- and third-grade years, she continues with additional interventions such as reading recovery. Roger describes his daughter as very self-aware of her strengths as well as her areas of weakness. She constantly compares herself to her peers, and in a high-performing district with affluent peers, her shortcomings foster a "never-ending cycle" of internal narratives where she calls herself stupid constantly. It is also around this time that Faith begins to explicitly name that she is a Black child with two White parents, and this is an additional source of confusion and frustration for her. Roger and his husband actively seek our diverse peer relationships for their children, as well as adult friendships with Black women, so that Faith has access to a racial affinity–based support group. For her fourth-grade year, her educational placement through the IEP is changed to a therapeutic special day class to support her social-emotional, behavioral, and academic needs in a smaller classroom setting with more adult assistance in the classroom, including mental health check-ins embedded throughout the day. The IEP team considers that Faith has shown little growth in terms of academic progress, and believes that this new environment will meet her unique learning needs.

As Roger begins to describe the support available to Faith in this new placement, I realize that he is depicting a program similar to the classrooms in which I had spent my first five years of teaching. Once I had disclosed my experience in nonpublic schools (NPS) and therapeutic day classes (TDCs) to him, he expresses his dislike of a "chill out room," which he describes as "like a padded closet." Roger never alludes to Faith being physically restrained by staff, but knowing the sequence of events that most often results in students going to a chill out or "quiet room," the majority of students do not walk willingly into that tiny space. The pedagogy of pathologization represents what Annamma (2017) describes as the result of the hyperlabeling, hypervigilance, and hyperpunishment of dis/abled girls of color. I cannot resist making the connection between Faith's time at the "academy" and the experiences of the multiple-marginalized girls of color in juvenile detention facilities in Annamma's work.

"She became like a part of the family."

Despite the difficulties Roger and Jeff face with Faith's placement and her resistance to the behavioral interventions in her classroom, Roger speaks fondly about a caseworker he deals with on the East Coast, who provides the family with emails, quarterly updates, and reports. I clarify to ask if this caseworker is someone different from Faith's or Marcus's special education teacher, who will generally take on case management duties in our current district. Roger states that the caseworker is a member of the guidance counseling team, who will call him before IEP meetings to discuss his concerns and acts as an advocate for the family during the IEP meeting. This is a more personable touch than the principal directly calling when there is an issue, because she knows the family and has that prior relationship with them. Roger does admit, "It's hard having a parent who's also a teacher who knows the rules," and shares that communication with principals since returning to California a few years ago has been mixed. While Faith's current middle school principal is open, communicative, and collaborative in his problem-solving approach, he has issues with a previous administrator sharing confidential information to others. Roger expects honesty and collaboration when working with his children's school staff, and his caseworker from the East Coast sets a high standard for expectations.

"It's a whole new . . . something."

When a student who has an Individualized Education Plan moves to a different state, county, or even district, there is often some difficulty in interpreting the IEP to fit the mold of the services that are available within the new jurisdiction. This is not how the IEP was intended to be, as it takes the "i" (individualized) out of the plan; however, it is common practice nonetheless.

When I first meet Roger in the summer of 2018, he and his family are in the process of moving back to Northern California. Faith is entering fifth grade and Marcus is to begin fourth grade. I receive their IEP paperwork, and based on Faith's previous placement, propose the idea of a class run by the County Office of Education (COE) to Roger, at a K–8 school in a city in the northern part of the county. Roger does not feel comfortable with his daughter commuting more than thirty minutes by bus to school, so he requests an in-district placement instead. Faith is placed in a special day class (SDC) for students in grades three through five at a district elementary school. Roger raves about the school psychologist at this site, and the positive rapport she quickly develops with Faith. The SDC where she is placed is considered cross-categorical, meaning that students have a variety of unique learning needs. Whereas in her previous placement, all of the students receive special education under the eligibility criteria of emotionally disturbed, Faith now shares a class with students who are thought to have a disability that is considered mild to moderate. This designation is ambiguous; students who will fall into this category might include those designated as having a specific learning disability (SLD), other health impairment (OHI) such as attention deficit hyperactivity disorder (ADHD), and autism (AUT). This heterogeneous mix of students has a range of academic abilities, and Faith finds enjoyment in coaching and tutoring her classmates, and serves as a role model and peer buddy. With the assistance of the school psychologist, who also serves as her mental health clinician, Faith is able to slowly amend her internal narrative, and her self-esteem increases. During her fifth-grade year, Faith also begins to mainstream out into general education more, with the support of a classroom paraprofessional.

"What's going on?"

When moving back to California from the East Coast, Roger is most concerned about Faith's proper placement in elementary school because of her history in a restrictive setting. Although Marcus is considered a student who receives resource specialist (RSP) support in his previous district, the amount of minutes and percentages outlined in his IEP align more with what students in his new district generally receive in an SDC. Roger agrees that the two siblings should not be in the same classroom, and as a result, they are placed in different elementary schools altogether. Marcus is in a classroom with a makeup of students similar to that of his sister; however, Roger becomes quickly concerned when Marcus comes home and shares stories of the externalizing behaviors some of his peers exhibit while in class. Roger decides to take the year off from teaching in order to get both of the children transitioned successfully at their new schools, so he asks to observe Marcus's classroom. While he states that he is impressed with the number of adults supporting students in the room, there is too much talking for Marcus to fully concentrate. Roger advocates for Marcus to receive his services from the RSP teacher, so that Marcus can have a general education homeroom class. Marcus continues to maintain relationships with some of his peers from the SDC class, as building friendships is an area where he struggles. In addition to this, Roger advocates for Marcus to be retained in fourth grade so that he can have a year to catch up to his peers, something that the principal grants. Roger recounts how he successfully requests that Faith be retained in the fourth grade in her old district. Roger also recognizes his insider knowledge of the system since he is a teacher and how he benefits from his social and navigational capital.

Many times throughout our conversation, Roger refers to "the East Coast way" as a standard of how special education services should be explained and delivered. Roger feels that the children's previous district is always "one step ahead" in terms of planning; he feels that in this California school district "we're always trying to put out the fire versus preventing the fire from starting." Roger sees the need for more social groups and more support for students who need it. In comparison to the previous district, he feels that more students require additional assistance, including the need for special education services. The larger proportion of students requiring additional support is compounded by the turnover of staff within the district, especially among occupational therapists and mental health clinicians. Roger explains that

> it's all good, it is what it is. But there's a high turnover, so it's just getting to know new people year after year in the department, which is challenging for the kids. And I think it's challenging for the parents too, 'cause I get those requests by five different people every year. "Oh, can you give me your background of your child and when did they start. . . . What were their milestones?" I'm like, "Isn't that somewhere in the IEP? I've given you guys all of that. Don't come to me and ask me, 'When did she start talking?'" I don't know how many times I've filled out that paperwork, but it's just too much.

While some parents might see these attempts by new service providers as a means of building rapport, Roger views it as school staff "not having done their homework" and regards this with a certain degree of mistrust. He recalls several times where he receives draft reports with incorrect student names and pronouns. Being a part of the system himself, he then goes on to say how he understands that school staff are charged with large caseloads that prevent them from being as thorough as he would like under "the East Coast way."

"They've been her little cheerleaders."

After a rocky first three months in middle school, Faith has flourished in the sixth and seventh grades. Presently, she is participating in school via distance learning, and the lack of peer distractions has helped her focus on the task at hand. She has one period a day of specialized academic instruction (SAI) with a special education teacher. Faith's IEP team decides it would be best for her to remain on the SDC teacher's caseload because of the positive rapport Faith has with him as well as the paraprofessional who accompanies her to some of her academic classes. At the beginning of the year, with the third mental health clinician assigned to her case in as many years, Roger makes the decision to decline Educationally Related Mental Health Services (ERMHS). Roger does not feel that starting over with another clinician is worth the time and irritation the adjustment has on Faith and the rest of the family. In addition to this, Faith has expressed frustration with the change, and since she is currently at home, Roger feels he can assist her with managing her feelings.

"Race isn't something that I can just ignore."

Roger understands the importance of helping his daughter navigate her reality as a Black girl with two White dads. He stresses the importance of exposing both of his children to Black and African American history, so they have a deeper understanding of their heritage. Roger reminds Faith about the power of being able to code switch language and tone depending on her surroundings, and holds up Michelle Obama as an ideal of Black womanhood. When the family decides to move back to California, they make the conscious decision to move to a diverse community that is close to Jeff's job. While the city in which Faith's and Marcus's schools are located is diverse, less than 1 percent of students enrolled in the district identify as Black. The majority of Black students in Northern California attend schools that Love (2019) calls "apartheid schools," where the main factor in their segregation is income disparity caused by institutional racism in government policy, real estate, and educational inequity.

"Switching the IEP meeting."

The last portion of my dialogue with Roger is centered on problem-solving issues he encounters as a parent of two children with IEPs. Roger feels very strongly that, in their present format, IEP meetings cannot meet the needs and concerns of parents. He states, "Because what you don't want is just parents leaving an IEP and just stewing and so angry, and then they're upset, and then that just creates tension where maybe you don't need tension."

Roger shares his own vignettes about leaving IEP meetings feeling upset after feeling like school staff disregard his concerns or do not actively seek his input when proposing important changes to the IEP documents. He also shares that certain staff have begun to talk over or interrupt his statements, which produces a silencing effect on the meeting.

Some of the recommendations that Roger proposes during our conversation are:

- Send drafts of the IEP home in advance so that parents have an opportunity to read them and bring questions to the meeting.
- Before the IEP, ask parents how and to what extent they want information presented in the meeting.
- Provide a parent portal for SEIS (Special Education Information System), the special education database used by the majority of school districts in California, so parents have a digital means of viewing their child's IEP.
- Share digital versions of IEPs after the meeting. Roger questions how putting a printed version of an IEP in a child's backpack is more secure than sending a portable document format (PDF) directly to a parent.
- Present an option to keep IEP meetings virtual at parent request after students have returned to in-person learning post–COVID-19.
- Prepare a pamphlet with information about outside organizations that parents can access with questions about special education. Some of this information is already available in the "Notice of Procedural Safeguards" presented to parents at the beginning of every IEP meeting; however, it is a lengthy document that many parents have not had time to fully review.
- Offer an anonymous post-IEP survey via Google Forms asking parents to rate their satisfaction and understanding of their child's IEP meeting. This can be used as an accountability tool for teachers and team members in their continued work with families.
- Provide access to and information about nondistrict parent support groups. For example, I share some of the work that our district's SEDAC (Special Education District Advisory Council) does and how outreach for parents has proceeded over recent months.

GLORIA AND TONY

Gloria and Tony are Filipino parents with two children: a daughter, Marie, who is currently in the fourth grade, and a seventh-grade son, Jeremy. Marie had previously received speech and language services from preschool through second grade. Jeremy is eligible for special education services under the categories autism (AUT) and speech and language impairment (SLI). I was part of Jeremy's IEP team during his third- through fifth-grade years.

Gloria and Tony have been active members of their son's IEP meetings and will request that they record the meetings so they can review the draft IEP again at home with the recording at hand. My first interaction with this family was at the beginning of Jeremy's third-grade year when he entered the school district. I sat next to Gloria and Tony in a conference room at Jeremy's elementary school. Tony took a two-inch binder out of a bag and placed it on the table. A photo of their son, smiling widely, was in the transparent sleeve at the front of the binder. Tony opened the binder and showed off some of Jeremy's work samples, some other family photos, and then took out the most recent IEP that they used as a reference with the new team, cross-referencing everything that was being proposed, added, or removed from the document. As a district employee who does not get to interact with students as frequently as I would like, this gesture grounded and reminded me that Jeremy is the reason we convene our meetings. Each year, Gloria and Tony update Jeremy's photo in the front of the binder, and they have now graduated to a thicker binder. Without fail, Gloria would always leave me a small holiday present at the front desk of the district office, even after I was no longer a part of their son's IEP team. Both English and Tagalog are spoken in the home. Gloria can carry on conversations in English; however, she often will turn to her husband and ask for a Tagalog translation when she requires assistance in understanding what is being said.

"We are so proud of our boy."

Sitting at my desk with the designated Zoom meeting open, waiting for the pop-up announcing that Gloria and Tony are waiting to be admitted to the virtual space, to my surprise, I see the name "Jeremy" pop up instead. I wait for my guest to join, and then turn on their video. Just as I suspect, Jeremy, joined by his father, appears on my screen. Jeremy, prompted by his father, Tony, exclaims, "Hello, Mrs. Vogel!" It has been quite a while since I have seen Jeremy, who now sports the beginnings of a mustache. He helps his father log onto Zoom and, after telling me about his day at school, goes into the other room to play *Minecraft*.

Tony is soon accompanied by his wife, Gloria, and we exchange pleasantries. Gloria is an extremely sweet woman, and asks me how school is going and what working from home is like. The warmth I feel when I was a member of Jeremy's IEP team returns, and I remember just how much I enjoyed working with this family.

Gloria and Tony's love for their son is immediately apparent within minutes of talking with them. They describe him as a happy, jolly, sociable, and outgoing young man. He loves trains and public transportation and has aspirations of being a conductor for BART, or a coal train driver, but as Tony explains with a laugh, "That's not really that feasible these days." Jeremy loves collecting maps from train and subway systems around the world and had planned a New York City adventure to ride the subway and visit Times Square for the New Year's Eve ball drop. Unfortunately, with COVID, this trip was delayed; Jeremy was able to visit New York for his middle school graduation in June 2022.

"We can see more potential in him."

As a seventh grader, Jeremy is enrolled in general education math, social studies, technology, and physical education. He takes English language arts, English language development, and science as part of the special day class (SDC) cohort with other seventh and eighth graders. Jeremy has the support of a trained behavioral therapist (BT) who utilizes strategies outlined in his behavior intervention plan (BIP). His BT accompanies him to his classes in the general education setting and supports him while he is in the SDC class, but to a lesser extent due to the smaller class size and knowledge of the teacher. Gloria and Tony express that they are extremely satisfied with Jeremy's current course load and their push for more mainstreaming time, which increases as he moves up in grade. While he has the occasional challenge, the teachers and staff at his middle school are accommodating and communicative with them, updating them on his progress or if adjustments need to be made to their delivery of instruction and expectations.

"We were so excited with our newborn."

Tony and Gloria describe the joy they feel when Jeremy is born. However, along with the joy comes trepidation and uncertainty. As a first child, they have no other example to compare him in terms of growth and development. In addition to this, they both live in Northern California, far away from their family in the Philippines. Gloria recounts the hours she spends on the phone with her mother, sisters, and aunts in the Philippines, asking them about childhood developmental milestones and what those benchmarks look like. Gloria and Tony begin to take their son to classes and group play at Gymboree to get a better understanding of how Jeremy's development compares to other children his age. Tony recalls noticing that around the age of one, Jeremy was often playing by himself in the corner while other children were beginning to experiment with cooperative play and games. "I wasn't sure entirely," he says, "but that was kind of the first warning sign."

"Hey, Doctor, you know there's something wrong."

As Jeremy turns one and a half, he has yet to develop any words and will babble and make noises when his parents are around. Tony shares that the family pediatrician has not made them aware of First Five California, a state sponsored organization that works to promote awareness about the importance of early childhood development and intervention. He states that if he and his wife had received access to that information it would have provided them with a better understanding of how to advocate for their son with the pediatrician. Tony and Gloria, relatively on their own in this country, do not benefit from extended community and networks that may alert them to resources.

When Jeremy is around two years of age, Tony and Gloria begin to express concerns about their son's development to their pediatrician. Their worries are disregarded by the doctor; Gloria says that he tells them not to worry because children begin speaking at different ages. The doctor says to wait until Jeremy is approaching his third birthday and to seek an evaluation for special education from their local school district. The doctor does not provide referrals to medical specialists at this time.

"We're not in the profession to know the development of our child."

As suggested by their pediatrician, Tony and Gloria request an assessment for Jeremy close to his third birthday. The school district team consists of a psychologist, an occupational therapist, and a speech-language pathologist. Each of the team members comes into the family's home to conduct their assessments and observe Jeremy's behavior. When Gloria expresses concern that Jeremy is not stacking blocks during play, the psychologist tells her, "Don't worry, he's fine." Instead of discussing Gloria's astute observations, the psychologist dismisses the family's knowledge of their son. Tony estimates that each of the assessors takes about one hour with Jeremy. He questions if this is enough time to get adequate information about his child, but, at the time, Tony does not believe it is appropriate for him to critique the methods used by professionals.

After the assessments are complete, a meeting is held to review the reports and determine eligibility for special education services. All three assessors determine that Jeremy does not meet the eligibility requirements for an IEP, and therefore receives a DNQ (do not qualify). Neither Tony nor Gloria feel that this is a satisfactory outcome, and once again return to their pediatrician requesting assistance in receiving a medical-based intervention or diagnosis. This time, they are put on a waiting list to see a developmental pediatrician and other specialists at a local institution.

"I think this book is telling me that our son has autism."

After Jeremy is found ineligible for special education services by the school district and is referred for additional assessment by his doctor, the family temporarily relocates to Australia to assist with extended familial duties. Gloria and Tony are given an estimate of five to seven months for Jeremy's name to move to the top of the assessment list. Tony begins to educate himself on early childhood development, and begins visiting local libraries. It is during this time that he finds a book on a shelf that seems to describe many of the things he is observing with his son. While he is not able to recall the name of the book, he clearly has some short passages committed to memory. "All of these characteristics they are talking about, it is almost as if they have observed my son play. That book spoke to me." After this revelation, Tony is convinced that Jeremy is a child with autism spectrum disorder (ASD).

Jeremy's name comes up earlier than expected on the waiting list, so after a little more than three months, the family moves back to the United States and meets with the specialists at the university hospital. They are assisted in receiving a referral for the Golden Gate Regional Center (GGRC), a nonprofit organization serving children and families with developmental disabilities in several Northern California counties. Tony's suspicions are confirmed when Jeremy does indeed receive a medical diagnosis of autism and, additionally, qualifies for support and resources from GGRC. With this additional knowledge and a note from a doctor at the university hospital questioning the validity of the first round of testing, Gloria and Tony return to the school district and request a second assessment.

Gloria and Tony's experience with the school-based assessment team is significantly different the second time around. Once again, the psychologist comes into the home to conduct some observations, but the majority of the assessments are conducted on a school campus. Each assessor takes several hours to complete their portion of the testing, and Gloria and Tony receive draft copies of the full report before the meeting. The psychologist provides them with information about the difference between a medical-based diagnosis of autism and school-based eligibility and services. Tony learns about the *Diagnostic and Statistical Manual of Mental Disorders* (*DSM*), which at that time was in its fourth edition. Tony purchases a copy of the *DSM* for his own reference so he can "speak the same language" as the school professionals. Tony further explains, "We missed the opportunity for Jeremy to receive early intervention because of the long period of waiting and assessment, and I wasn't going to allow that again in the future."

Jeremy does qualify for special education services under the eligibility category of AUT, as well as SLI, the same two categories he receives services under today. It is important to note that while many students with autism also receive language and speech, it is not an automatic dual eligibility. The school district offers placement in one of their SDCs, which serves eight students and is staffed by a special education teacher and a paraeducator. Gloria and Tony relay this information with a sense of relief and state that Jeremy "finally, he got what he needed" to thrive and grow.

"We're just immigrants here; we don't know the system."

As Jeremy transitions to kindergarten, he begins to exhibit some challenging behaviors in school. He begins receiving applied behavior analysis (ABA) therapy at home, and Gloria and Tony ask for behavioral interventions to create consistency across the home–school settings. In passing, the school psychologist mentions a classroom on a district campus that serves students on the autism spectrum with embedded ABA strategies and a lower student-to-teacher ratio that may be an option for Jeremy. Tony perceives this conversation as an invitation to go visit the classroom in anticipation of his son changing classrooms. The day after he goes to visit, he recalls receiving a "scathing" email from the school psychologist and the director of special education, stating that Tony is not permitted to observe the classroom further, and that the district will not be recommending a change of placement for Jeremy. Tony expounds on the incident further when he states, "Whatever the authority will tell us, we will just follow, and that's one thing that sometimes. . . . And we're not very vocal, we're not very vocal. We don't know how the system works because we're just. . . . We're coming from. . . . We're immigrants, basically."

Several times through our conversation, Tony and Gloria emphasize that they went into this journey with complete trust in the professionals. Over time, this implicit trust is eroded by the dismissive and patronizing behaviors of doctors and school staff. It was devastating to hear the ways in which these parents are not guided according to our ethical and moral duties as educators. When this trust is broken, it does irreparable harm to the working relationship that must exist in order for a team to work together effectively. Tony clearly illustrates this when he declares, "We gave all our trust to them, and when that happened, I knew it was time to go." Tony cites the email from the director of special education as "the last straw" in a group of instances where he and his wife feel betrayed by school district staff. Because of the lack of support that Gloria and Tony feel from Jeremy's IEP team, they make the decision to move and rent an apartment in a neighboring city that has a better reputation for supporting students and families in special education.

"When will we find a good support plan for our son?"

Starting in first grade, Jeremy is enrolled in a special day class for students on the autism spectrum in his new district. Although the family only moves a few blocks from their previous residence, their new apartment falls under the jurisdiction of a different district than he was previously enrolled in. His teacher, along with his speech language pathologist and occupational therapist, communicate with Gloria and Tony on a regular basis and utilize many of the interventions recommended by his home ABA clinician. In the middle of the school year, Jeremy begins eloping from the classroom and manages to run off school property a few times. In addition to this, when he becomes overwhelmed with sensory stimulation, he disrobes in the middle of class and needs redirection to a separate space to deescalate. Despite these occurrences, the new district denies assessment for in-school ABA services, citing that Jeremy's behavior is being managed by the supports currently in place in the classroom. Jeremy's parents, as well as some of the school staff, disagree with this rationale. Gloria wonders, "Was it because of money? I do not know. All I know is that he needed something else, the teacher said he needed something else, but the district said no." By acknowledging the limitations of district resources, Gloria demonstrates an understanding that while schools are tasked with providing students with the services they need, their spending is often constrained by budgets and line items.

At the end of Jeremy's second-grade year, Gloria and Tony had "fulfilled the American dream" with the purchase of a condo in a nearby city, and the family switches districts once again.

"It's not gonna be cheap, but if it's what we have to do, so be it."

Jeremy and his younger sister, Marie, start their third and kindergarten years, respectively, at a new school in their new district. It is at this point in Jeremy's educational journey that I first become involved with his IEP team. Based on his IEP, Jeremy is placed in a special day class for students in grades one through three who are designated as having a mild to moderate disability. Tony and Gloria immediately develop a positive rapport with Jeremy's new teacher, who is Filipina, and they communicate in Tagalog. Gloria calls her "an angel, a wonderful teacher," and Jeremy makes academic and behavioral progress throughout the school year. For his fourth-grade year, he ages out of that class and moves into a similar classroom for students in grades four and five at the same campus. In this new environment, he begins to exhibit the same behaviors from years past, eloping from the classroom and school campus, and removing his clothes when he is overly agitated. Jeremy's teacher, who is new to the campus, consults with his previous classroom team, but the behaviors become more intense.

The school psychologist conducts a functional behavioral assessment (FBA) and develops an updated behavior intervention plan (BIP) in collaboration with the IEP team. It is at this time that Jeremy's home ABA team and school team begin to meet twice monthly to calibrate strategies and support. Based on the results of the FBA, a classroom aide is assigned to individually support Jeremy at identified times throughout the day. However, the classroom is also short staffed, so this creates additional scheduling barriers and the support is not always consistently implemented. Both parents share that they feel let down by the district, because the classroom team is resistant to implementing the BIP. "It's like they were waiting for something to happen and then blame my son instead of using the plan." By placing the onus on the student and parent, staff are able to extricate themselves from responsibility. It is around this time that Gloria and Tony hire an advocate to help them navigate the special education process.

When I ask Gloria and Tony how they had found the advocate who has been working with them for the past four years, they share that they were referred to her after a conversation with a mother in the waiting room of the ABA clinic that Jeremy attends. This mother raves about the progress that her high school–aged son has been making since retaining the advocate's services. Tony relays that "she said in order for you to get the services that you need, you need to get a good advocate." I share with Gloria and Tony that upon seeing her walk in with them to an IEP meeting that I too had felt some relief, particularly that she provides some extra push in showing the teams how vital it is to follow plans. Gloria refers to the advocate as "an angel with a warm heart," and that she is worth the expense they invest in her services.

The remainder of Jeremy's fourth-grade year proves to be a challenge, but with a change of teacher for his fifth-grade year, the tone of meetings changes. Jeremy now has an experienced teacher with a background in behavior and positive reinforcement, who gladly supports the BIP implementation. Jeremy also qualifies for full-day support from a behavioral therapist (BT) from a nonpublic agency, who has more targeted knowledge around behavior than a traditional classroom paraprofessional. The team sees Jeremy's behaviors decrease in both intensity and duration, and he begins to attend mainstream classes outside of his special day class more frequently.

When it comes time for Jeremy's transition to middle school, there is some trepidation on my part, specifically because of the progress he has made over the past year. Jeremy is offered placement in a special day class at the middle school closest to his home, in line with providing students services in the least restrictive environment (LRE). It is unknown who the special day class teacher will be, as the teacher of record is leaving at the end of the year. The IEP team holds two meetings at the new school site, and a plan is put into place to continue all of Jeremy's current services and supports. Right before the beginning of the school year, Jeremy's fifth-grade teacher moves up to the sixth- to seventh-grade class where he is to begin in a matter of weeks. It is a pleasant surprise for both his parents and alleviates most of my anxiety about the change. Jeremy's teacher is described by his parents as "a second advocate" and is not intimidated by speaking up for what she believes he needs in meetings. At this point, I transition off the IEP team, as his new school was not one that I support.

"He has become a better person."

As a seventh grader, Jeremy has maintained straight As and has been on the honor roll for the past year. Tony believes that this is in part to "unlocking his potential" and shares that the beginning of Jeremy's middle school experience is challenging, especially with changing classes daily and electives rotating on a quarterly basis. The key to success is consistency, specifically that Jeremy's BT has remained the same since fifth grade, as well as the team meetings between the home ABA team and the school behavior team. With the transition to distance learning in March 2020 due to the COVID-19 pandemic, Jeremy has been supported virtually by his BT in his classes.

After two years, Jeremy has a new special education teacher and case manager, but she has continued the level of communication and support that Gloria and Tony have become accustomed to. Jeremy is eagerly waiting for in-person learning to commence, so he can finally meet his teacher face to face and catch up with his classmates. Gloria shares with a bright smile that Jeremy takes every opportunity he can to visit the school campus, including material pick-up day and picture day. She adds, "He even wanted to go to the retake day, but I said no because his seventh-grade photo is so handsome." Just so I had photo evidence, she goes to retrieve the photo so I can see for myself. Grinning from ear to ear, with lustrous shoulder-length hair, her son is almost her twin. When I remark on this, she begins to giggle. "Well, yes, but he has his father's mustache," making a finger motion of what she then describes as a waxing strip. For a family that has experienced so much heartache and frustration, this is a perfect way to wrap up our conversation so Gloria can begin to prepare dinner. At the end of our conversation, Tony shares that he knows how to log into Zoom, but his son wanted to show him how. "I'm not going to deny him that." With that, our call ends.

TOMAS

Tomas is a Spanish-speaking Mexican man with seven children: three daughters of adult age, a seventeen-year-old son, a fifteen-year-old daughter, and a thirteen-year-old son. His eldest son, Isaiah, is eligible for special education services under the category multiple disability (MD). Isaiah attends a special day class (SDC) as an eleventh grader in the local high school district. I first became acquainted with Tomas and his family as the program specialist assigned to his school site and was part of his IEP team during his seventh- and eighth-grade years. Tomas was able to attend IEPs occasionally, when his work schedule allowed. I recall a few instances where he was able to phone into the meeting during a break time so that he could listen and participate. Since the beginning of the pandemic in March of 2020, Isaiah has participated minimally in his education program, but continues to receive his CCS (California Children's Services) physical therapy in person, at home. Spanish is the primary language spoken in the home; both Tomas and his wife participate in Isaiah's IEP meetings with the assistance of a Spanish interpreter. During our conversation, there were several times when he spoke briefly in English, and then switched back to Spanish.

"It's quite a large family, as you know."

Tomas always speaks lovingly about his children. Whether it is sharing photos of his daughter's artwork or his other daughter at army basic training before and after IEP meetings, he takes pride in his children's accomplishments. Having most of his family living at home for the past nine months is proving to be a bit of a challenge, especially when finding a quiet space to talk. During our conversation, background chatter, laughter, and the occasional raised voice distract him for a few seconds at a time. He turns around a few times to make sure that everything is alright before settling back into our dialogue.

With the exception of an intervention plan his daughter has for one semester that helps her catch up on missing work, six of his seven children have had few issues with school. "They have all done really well. My wife and I are very proud of them," Tomas states, smiling. "Even Isaiah, we are proud of him too. He is our special baby boy." The day that we schedule to speak is Isaiah's seventeenth birthday, and Tomas's wife and daughters are baking a cake for him. "He's almost a man; he will get to vote next year," he laughs. Almost as if on cue, loud vocalizations can be heard from the other room. "He knows we're talking about him," Tomas states, again with a wide smile. "I love my special boy."

"Developmentally, he's a toddler at best."

Isaiah is born with several significant health and developmental issues: microcephaly, which has resulted in global cognitive and physical impairments; sclerocornea, an eye condition where the cornea lacks a distinct barrier and leads to near blindness; and spastic cerebral palsy, which causes a stiffening of the body's muscles and causes movement to be difficult and slow. In addition to this, Tomas states that Isaiah also has sensory disorder, which affects his ability to process sensory information and input. According to Tomas, Isaiah is "totally dependent" on his parents and siblings for basic needs, including feeding and diapering. Tomas describes how Isaiah will move around the house on his hands and knees since it is faster than walking. He knows what his boundaries are and has developed a "circuit around the house he likes to travel to see his favorite spots." When furniture is moved around the house, it often causes Isaiah to become irritable; he will cry and tantrum for upward of two hours until things are put back to their original locations. With some of his adult children moving back into the family home during the COVID-19 pandemic, this creates disruptions to Isaiah's routine on a consistent basis. Tomas shrugs and states, "In a lot of ways he is just like a regular moody teenager. Emotions here, emotions there."

While Isaiah is nonverbal, he is extremely vocal and will make noise for a good portion of his waking hours. Tomas believes that he "likes to hear himself" but is unsure if Isaiah is attempting to communicate with others. Isaiah loves music and will grab a phone or iPad that is playing music and hold it close to his ear to listen. The family monitors Isaiah around electronic devices out of concern that his hearing will be damaged if he has a speaker too close or inside his ear. Because of this safety concern, Isaiah is not permitted to use earbuds or headphones.

I ask Tomas if Isaiah has been evaluated for alternative and augmentative communication (AAC), to which he replies that there had been some type of assessment when Isaiah was in elementary school, but it was determined that a high-tech device would be inappropriate for his son. "Based on his cognitive level, as well as his blindness, he couldn't really use it when they tried," he explains. Tomas shares that everyone has a slightly different way of communicating with Isaiah, "their own sort of Morse code with him." The physical therapist teaches Isaiah basic American Sign Language (ASL) for "thank you" and "more," but Isaiah has not yet learned any other additional signs. Additionally, Tomas is the only member of the family who Isaiah consistently listens to. This is chalked up to "the power of Dad," a phrase that Marcy, Isaiah's wife, coined several years ago.

Isaiah's sclerocornea results in a significant visual impairment to the point where Tomas believes his son is only able to see colors and the shapes of objects within close proximity. Tomas observes him focusing on the changing colors of the screen saver on his sister's iPhone and Chromebook, but Isaiah does not engage with TV or videos on the computer. "A teenager who doesn't like YouTube!" Tomas exclaims in English, with laughter.

"He's had an IEP since day one."

As Isaiah is born with significant health and developmental issues, he begins receiving early intervention services at a very young age. Tomas is not able to recall all of the various therapists and service providers who support Isaiah and the rest of the family, but says that the house has been a "revolving door" of people coming in and out to visit, observe, and work with Isaiah. When evaluating the quality of services over the past seventeen years, Tomas simply states that there have been "ups and downs" but that, overall, he and his family are pleased with the professionals and services that are offered to Isaiah. When the time comes to move Isaiah's services from an Individualized Family Service Plan (IFSP) to an IEP just before his third birthday, Tomas recalls that the school district team "welcomed them with open arms" and that "there wasn't much to it other than getting to know the people that were gonna be taking care of him." In terms of school readiness, Isaiah is completely reliant on others for all tasks, including feeding. Since entering school, Isaiah has learned to independently complete some basic daily living skills, such as washing his hands, using a straw to drink water from a cup, and handling a spoon to eat cereal and other "mushy" foods, which he prefers.

Tomas speaks fondly of Isaiah's teachers and staff through his elementary and middle school years. Isaiah develops a deep connection with several of the paraprofessionals in his classes, and cries when he leaves school. "I think he missed them when he went home." As Isaiah grows up and ages out of classrooms, Tomas feels that the elementary school district is able to provide him with a classroom that is appropriate for his particular learning needs. He states, "It's always been pretty easy to place him where he needs to be." However, with Isiah's transition to high school, there is a slight shift in his father's perception of what is an appropriate classroom for his son.

"It's not designed for kids like him."

Currently, Isaiah attends his local high school and is enrolled in a classroom designated for students with moderate to severe disabilities. There are twelve students in the class and generally four to six adults supporting the students, including the special education teacher, who serves as Isaiah's case manager. Isaiah has special circumstance instructional assistance (SCIA) written into his IEP; however, the paraprofessionals rotate their support of students throughout the day. His school day ends around noon; at that time, he is transported to a program with hands-on activities and outings.

Tomas expresses some concern that Isaiah's current classroom is not specifically set up for students who are mobile. The other students in Isaiah's class all use a wheelchair as their primary means of movement. Isaiah utilizes a wheelchair during the school day, but he is able to get up and move around. The center-based classroom is set up where the teachers rotate to the students, minimizing the opportunity for movement, which has frustrated Isaiah. Tomas does not know if there is a classroom more appropriate for Isaiah in another school in the district, but when I ask, he states he would not want him moved at this point in his schooling because his son is "comfortable" with the teachers and other staff.

"There's a waiting list, and apparently it orbits the Earth a couple of times."

Isaiah is eligible to receive occupational therapy (OT) services since he entered the school system at the age of three. However, Tomas relays that Isaiah has not had a consistent OT provider for more than a year at a time. This creates issues with communication as well as rapport with both Isaiah and the family. In addition to this, Isaiah qualifies for OT through CCS, but this service is inconsistently delivered. Tomas sums up his frustration by stating, "His doctor said, 'Yes, he needs it.' The insurance says, 'Yes, we agree with you. He needs it.' Finding someone to do it is the challenge."

Staffing is a significant challenge in the field of special education, and this creates barriers for students' progress. There have been some programs that incentivize a switch of careers, but more needs to be done to meet the needs of our students and families.

"There really isn't much he can do right now."

Like the majority of children around the world during the COVID-19 pandemic, Isaiah is not attending a brick-and-mortar school at this time. While distance learning is working for Tomas's two other school-aged children, Isaiah is not able to participate in class meetings and activities, mostly due to his near blindness and his developmental level. Tomas and his wife arrange to record a video of Isaiah participating in physical therapy with his therapist from CCS, who has been entering the home since mid-October. His teacher will also communicate with Tomas's wife, Marcy, every other week over the phone to suggest activities and exercises for Isaiah to complete.

Tomas shares his experience with one of Isaiah's new service providers this year, which he describes as "a little bit of miscommunication." He is unable to identify what particular service this professional was providing to Isaiah, but states she contacts Marcy at the beginning of the school year to set up times for Isaiah to log onto Zoom and participate in therapy. Tomas feels that the therapist's expectations for Isaiah's participation are unrealistic and demonstrate that she had not reviewed his file prior to communicating with the family. He elaborates by saying,

> It would be easy enough to make the connection that he [Isaiah] is part of a special needs class and rather than make the assumption that reviewing lessons is something that he can even do, rather reach out and get clarification first, and then work with us as the parents, to determine what's reasonable and what isn't.

Tomas captures the travesty of the power imbalance between the educator and the devoted parent. The educator's dismissal of familial knowledge and familial capacity to co-construct a supportive learning environment invisibilizes both Isaiah and his family. This scenario visibilizes the unexamined assumptions regarding culturally and linguistically diverse families, and the devaluing of Isaiah's potential. The implicit message is for families to accept that professionals know best. Tomas's narrative is an indictment of the prescriptive medical model of disability, which fails to provide spaces for families to collaborate on how to best serve their children.

In this instance, Tomas is simply asking school staff to consult with them and get a better understanding of their child's abilities and needs before making unilateral decisions about delivery of services. This initial contact to families solidifies working relationships and reduces the possibility of situations where miscommunication abounds.

"It's never a situation where we feel our input isn't welcomed."

Tomas is able to attend IEP meetings for Isaiah when time permits around his work schedule. For Isaiah's annual IEP, which is held in October,

Tomas is able to participate "in person" over Zoom for the first time in several years. Before this, he most often phones into the meeting where he is put on speakerphone so he can both listen and speak. Marcy, Tomas's wife and Isaiah's mother, has attended the IEPs in person for as long as her son has been in school. She has more flexible work hours, so it is a "tag team effort" for the couple.

Since Isaiah began high school, Tomas has seen a plateau in his son's abilities. He states that Isaiah's team of doctors determine that he has developed as much as he is able to. Isaiah's IEP goals change slightly over the past few years, but mainly focus on daily living skills, with small increments of expected improvement. I ask Tomas if Isaiah's school team and medical team collaborate on a consistent basis, or if any of Isaiah's doctors attend his IEP meetings. At first, Tomas is not sure, but after clarifying with Marcy, he clarifies that the last time a doctor attended an IEP was in kindergarten.

"Negotiating the best deal possible."

During our discussion about his experiences with the IEP process, Tomas shares that he has developed a strategy for ensuring that Isaiah receives adequate services from the school-based professionals. This involves developing "high bids" for services such as speech and physical therapy, and then negotiating with the rest of the IEP team for an appropriate frequency and duration of said services. He further elaborates that

> if I go into a meeting with ninety minutes of speech as an ideal and they offer sixty, I can counter them and try to get seventy-five. I never expect to get the full ninety, but if I set the bar high, it can't be lowered that much.

I find this approach surprising, especially since Tomas shares his overall satisfaction with the IEP process for his son. I follow up with Tomas after the dialogue to ask him if the school-based IEP team had ever objected to the stance or method he takes in advocating for services for Isaiah. Tomas replies with,

> No, they know me by now and my style. Sometimes the team members will ask me now what I recommend for services before they propose their times. They will laugh a bit, but I know they

take it seriously. No one has ever fought me on it, but I have to keep doing it because I am so used to it.

After receiving Tomas's follow-up, I realize that this act of negotiation is not rooted in antagonism. Instead, this appears to be the outlet for Tomas to act as collaborator in the IEP meetings. At the same time, this demonstrates that Tomas is confident in his ability to act as a member of the IEP team. This is more in line with the remainder of his narrative.

"Twenty-two is where everything changes."

Since our dialogue is conducted on Isaiah's birthday, I ask Tomas if the family and school team have begun to discuss what life after secondary school will look like. Tomas states that he and his wife have had some anxiety over Isaiah turning eighteen in late 2021; however, they have been receiving guidance and support from the Regional Center, as well as some doctors, in completing the extensive paperwork required. Tomas expresses that "this is the first real new thing that we've encountered since we initially got him set up for everything."

Students that qualify for IEPs are entitled to school-based services until the age of twenty-two. Tomas shares that post–high school life has been discussed in Isaiah's IEPs for the past few years, including a "university" program for students ages eighteen to twenty-two at another local high school. Isaiah will receive a certificate of completion when he leaves high school, as his curriculum is heavily modified and does not meet California's A-G requirements for a diploma. The "university" program is a similar program to the one Isaiah is currently enrolled in, the main difference being that it is for older students.

POST-DIALOGUE REFLECTION

In the three years that I have known him, Roger has developed a reputation among staff for being firm with the expectations he has for his children's services, but understanding that systems are complex and that change takes time. He clearly communicates what he wants and has been willing to work in collaboration with IEP teams. It would be remiss of me to forget his ability to work with the system is due in part to his membership *in* the system, with the navigational capital that he has attained along the way. Rogers's openness during our conversation, especially his ability to express displeasure with staff actions or behavior, is situated in his positionality as an educated, cisgender, White male.

Returning to the subject of restraint and seclusion in schools that came up during my dialogue with Roger, the death of thirteen-year-old Max Benson in 2018 at a California nonpublic school due to prolonged prone restraint (Prince & Gothberg, 2019) occurred less than two months before the enactment of AB2657 (Assembly Bill 2657), also known as the Weber Bill. AB2657 explicitly states that physical or mechanical restraints are to be used only when a student's behavior poses "a clear and present danger of serious physical harm" to themselves or others that cannot be controlled by a less restrictive intervention (AB 2657, 2018). LEAs and county offices of education are responsible for providing training for staff in de-escalation techniques for students with challenging behavior. Any use of physical restraint is to be used as a last resort and must be documented and reviewed to reflect on how to further minimize placing hands on students. I have personal experience with restraint and seclusion in schools, as I worked in two nonpublic schools in the San Francisco Bay Area in the early 2000s that were somewhat liberal in their use of both practices. While staff received training on how to safely contain a student, the emphasis was on controlling the student's actions, not on assisting them with processing the feelings that lead to the behavior.

The ease with which Gloria, Tony, and I fall into conversation about their journey makes me miss working with them on a consistent basis. I was especially delighted to see Jeremy so grown up. The persistence and resiliency that Gloria and Tony demonstrate over the years in order to get an effective plan enacted for their son is both inspiring and frustrating at the same time. Providing Jeremy with a positive learning environment should not take multiple requests for support and relocating to different school districts. I am extremely grateful that not only do Gloria and Tony have the resources to retain an advocate but they also found one who is knowledgeable and a collaborative partner with the existing team. My experience working with the advocate retained by Gloria and Tony contrasts sharply with other times when advocates have taken an adversarial stance toward the teachers and other professionals on the IEP team. While their advocate treats all members of the IEP team with respect, I have encountered advocates hired by families who discredit the work teams have undertaken and thus create additional barriers to effective solutions. Parents and families deserve to have partners who work for them, as well as for the betterment of students.

While I had the assistance of a Spanish language interpreter, Tomas spends about half of the conversation speaking to me in English, asking clarifying questions to the interpreter when he wants to find the word in English he was looking for. I was surprised by the level of conversational English he has, as I had only interacted with him with full use of an interpreter in the past. Tomas has a cheerful disposition the entire conversation, making jokes and keeping the mood light. At one point, Isaiah crawls into the room Tomas is in and sits on the bed near his father. He begins to make humming sounds while we are speaking. Tomas stops the conversation briefly, asks the interpreter to speak, and then asks me to speak. After we stop talking, Isaiah's humming starts again. "I think he likes your voice," is the observation Tomas makes. Isaiah stays with his father for about ten minutes and then goes back to crawling about the house.

Important Reminders That Arise out of These Parent Dialogues

- It is vital for all special education professionals to understand that when families bring in outside assistance, that is a strong indicator that the school team needs to reexamine their work. It is not something to take personally, but reflect on your practices as a team.
- Be sure to have a clear understanding about communicating with advocates or attorneys that parents may choose to bring to meetings. Check with your principal or special education administrator about your school and district's policies.
- Do your research and gather background information before you reach out to a parent for the first time. Especially for parents who have children in upper elementary and beyond, cross-checking information you already have reviewed rather than going into a conversation as a blank slate can be helpful for busy parents.
- Provide clear timelines around when to expect communication and how you are best reached. Stick with these timelines; this is one of the guaranteed ways to establish rapport and trust with parents.

Reflection Questions

- Look up the IEP documents from another state and note the similarities and differences. How does this affect students and families who move? What can schools do to ease this transition?

- How much consideration is given to parent requests when weighed against school district and/or special education procedures?
- Discuss what "readiness" for mainstreaming and inclusion may look like for various members of the IEP team. How do school-based members of the team determine when a student should be included? What is the messaging we are sending to our families?
- What are the lessons learned from each of these three parent narratives? How are their experiences similar? How are they different? How did race, home language, and privilege affect their experience of the IEP process?

Group Activity

- Create timeline maps for the three parent narratives in this chapter. Make notation of where there was an inconsistency or disconnect between the parents and school or providers. Make notation of when there was harmony and collaboration between parents and school or providers. Share your timeline with a partner and discuss how each of these lynchpin moments positively or negatively affected the family experience.

CHAPTER 6

Lisa and Vanessa

....

LISA

Lisa is a European American woman with three children: a nonbinary college student, one daughter who is a high school senior, and a fourth-grade boy. Her son, Sam, is eligible for special education services under the categories emotional disturbance (ED) and speech and language impairment (SLI). Sam attends a nonpublic school (NPS), which is paid for by the district through his IEP. I have not had direct contact with Lisa or her family in a professional capacity until the beginning of this research. Lisa is a former special education teacher and now works at a local private university in their accessibility services division. With her background, Lisa has a deeper understanding of the IEP process than the majority of parents served by the district. Initially, her son was enrolled in a charter school and came to the district after the charter informed her that they were unable to serve Sam during his kindergarten year. Since then, Sam has attended the nonpublic school, which is a forty-five-minute drive from their home. Sam has been participating in distance learning since March of 2020 due to the COVID-19 pandemic, and has been receiving his academic instruction, emotional and behavioral support, and speech, occupational, and physical therapies remotely. Joel, Lisa's husband and Sam's dad, has been assisting Sam with distance learning.

"He's a complex dude."

Lisa and I meet over Zoom during the Thanksgiving break. She has graciously given up a portion of her Friday morning to talk with me about her son's journey in special education. Sam loves to read and his favorite subject in school is social studies. His school has adopted a supplemental

Lisa and Vanessa
Art by Chris Holland. Reprinted with permission.

history curriculum based on the Carmen Sandiego character, and Lisa raves at how engaging it is for Sam. "He just soaks it all in," she states. Academically, Sam is about a year and a half above his current grade level in both reading and writing, but struggles significantly with math. During distance learning, either Lisa or Joel spends the entirety of his math class next to him, encouraging him and providing support. This is similar to the assistance he receives when he is in school, where either the teacher or an aide has a supportive hand on his shoulder, encouraging him with motivation such as "come on" and "let's focus." In his free time, Sam enjoys playing Legos and *Minecraft*. "He's just a typicalish kid," states Lisa, "except he's been on an emotional roller coaster since a very early age. He's so intense, you can just see it." He currently receives treatment and services for clinical depression and generalized anxiety, as well as ADHD.

CHAPTER 6

Lisa and Vanessa

LISA

Lisa is a European American woman with three children: a nonbinary college student, one daughter who is a high school senior, and a fourth-grade boy. Her son, Sam, is eligible for special education services under the categories emotional disturbance (ED) and speech and language impairment (SLI). Sam attends a nonpublic school (NPS), which is paid for by the district through his IEP. I have not had direct contact with Lisa or her family in a professional capacity until the beginning of this research. Lisa is a former special education teacher and now works at a local private university in their accessibility services division. With her background, Lisa has a deeper understanding of the IEP process than the majority of parents served by the district. Initially, her son was enrolled in a charter school and came to the district after the charter informed her that they were unable to serve Sam during his kindergarten year. Since then, Sam has attended the nonpublic school, which is a forty-five-minute drive from their home. Sam has been participating in distance learning since March of 2020 due to the COVID-19 pandemic, and has been receiving his academic instruction, emotional and behavioral support, and speech, occupational, and physical therapies remotely. Joel, Lisa's husband and Sam's dad, has been assisting Sam with distance learning.

"He's a complex dude."

Lisa and I meet over Zoom during the Thanksgiving break. She has graciously given up a portion of her Friday morning to talk with me about her son's journey in special education. Sam loves to read and his favorite subject in school is social studies. His school has adopted a supplemental

Lisa and Vanessa
Art by Chris Holland. Reprinted with permission.

history curriculum based on the Carmen Sandiego character, and Lisa raves at how engaging it is for Sam. "He just soaks it all in," she states. Academically, Sam is about a year and a half above his current grade level in both reading and writing, but struggles significantly with math. During distance learning, either Lisa or Joel spends the entirety of his math class next to him, encouraging him and providing support. This is similar to the assistance he receives when he is in school, where either the teacher or an aide has a supportive hand on his shoulder, encouraging him with motivation such as "come on" and "let's focus." In his free time, Sam enjoys playing Legos and *Minecraft*. "He's just a typicalish kid," states Lisa, "except he's been on an emotional roller coaster since a very early age. He's so intense, you can just see it." He currently receives treatment and services for clinical depression and generalized anxiety, as well as ADHD.

"There were a few mishaps early on."

From an early age, Sam experiences a few incidents, which result in a delay of his speech and language skills. At the age of two years old, Sam is found to have impacted cerumen, or earwax, in his ear, which results in a temporary hearing loss of up to 50 percent. In order to correct this, he has tubes placed in his ear, which corrects the majority of the loss associated with the impaction. About a year later, he splits his front tooth after a fall on the playground and has it surgically removed. He goes without a front tooth for the next four years, and this affects his ability to form specific words and sounds, especially "th" words.

"This isn't autism . . . this is definitely something else."

Sam is enrolled in a private preschool, where the staff express concern regarding his difficulty transitioning from one activity to another, as well as some aggressive behaviors when presented with nonpreferred activities. Lisa states that Sam's behaviors at home are not a concern at this time. However, when he begins kindergarten, Sam begins to have significant meltdowns at home, tantruming when he is given a direction, and throwing toys at his parents and sisters. Lisa recounts one instance where Sam was hugging her and became so overstimulated that he bit her arm and broke the skin. However, Lisa immediately clarifies that "I wasn't mad at him because I understand. He was in this great mood and he was so excited."

Due to the escalation in Sam's behaviors, Lisa and Joel take Sam to his pediatrician, who refers them to a psychologist and a neurologist. Sam is assessed by these professionals, and is determined to have oppositional defiant disorder (ODD), as well as attention deficit hyperactivity disorder (ADHD). Sam is not found to have any learning disabilities at this time, primarily because it is extremely difficult to determine this in children so young. When speaking about Sam's medical diagnosis of ODD, Lisa states that she "never really agreed with it, and that's been really hard as parents." She is speaking to the social stigma tied to having a child identified with conditions related to emotional disturbance (ED), which is related to our society's lack of recognition and treatment for behavioral and mental health issues.

"There's nothing we can do; we've tried everything."

Sam's kindergarten school team sees an increase in behavior as well. Lisa recounts that she and Joel are called by the office on a daily basis to pick

Sam up from school. There are thirty students in his kindergarten class, which is staffed by a teacher and a teacher's assistant. While Sam has an IEP under the eligibility category SLI, due to his articulation, as well as receptive language delays, the school team does not move forward with developing a behavior intervention plan (BIP), or drafting goals related to behavior. The school calls for a meeting with both Lisa and Joel and they feel pressured to disenroll Sam. Lisa recalls how they "fought like crazy to keep him in a regular public school":

> They were stunned and I said, "You're telling me that in five months into the school year you've tried everything?" And they said, "Yes." I said, "Okay, where is his functional behavior assessment? Cause I never got one of those. Where's his evaluation by a school psychologist? Where is the behavior support plan?" I said, "Because I haven't seen or signed any of that. You're telling me you've done everything, but I highly doubt it."

At one point in the meeting, one of the school team members states that if Sam's behaviors continue, the police might need to be called to initiate a 5150 psychiatric hold. When I ask her for an example of the behaviors Sam exhibits that raise such concern, she states that he cries uncontrollably, hits his head on desks or hard surfaces, and makes self-harm statements. Even though the school sees behaviors that may necessitate a 5150 call to the police, it is not until Lisa requests additional assessment for special education services that the school psychologist becomes involved with Sam's case. The assessment report developed by the school team recommends that Sam be made eligible for special education services under ED, with SLI shifting to his secondary eligibility. While there is a special day class (SDC) on campus, the team does not recommend this as a potential placement for Sam, as he does not have a specific learning disability (SLD). Instead, they recommend placement at an NPS, a school setting where Sam has no opportunities to spend time with his peers in general education classes.

"I had to put my special education teacher hat on."

Lisa relays to me that she was instrumental in selecting the nonpublic school that Sam attends. Part of this is related to the way in which she utilizes her institutional knowledge of special education in assisting the district case manager in writing the IEP. Prior to Sam's birth, Lisa was a special education teacher for six years and is well versed in developing and writing IEPs. The special education teacher assigned to Sam is in her first year and sends home several drafts of the IEP prior to the meeting, which Lisa returns with corrections and suggestions. After the third draft, Lisa calls the teacher and meets her at school, where she walks the teacher through the IEP process. Lisa collaborates with the new teacher to ensure that certain verbiage is present in the documents so she ultimately is able to "get what Sam needed." One instance of this maneuvering is transportation. Lisa has concerns about Sam traveling to his new school with other students with emotional disturbance, who could potentially range in age from five to fourteen. Lisa prompts the teacher to write in the IEP that Sam requires individual transportation to school to prevent potential bullying or manipulation by other students. Lisa admits that this was "a really backwards process," and that she does not fault the special education teacher for her inexperience. Lisa fully recognizes that her position of privilege, based on professional knowledge, puts her at a distinct advantage over other parents, but she has no regrets about using her position to secure the services her son requires.

"It's phenomenal; I can't say enough good things."

Sam has been attending the same nonpublic school since the middle of his kindergarten year. His current classroom has eight other students in the third and fourth grades, and is staffed by a special education teacher, teacher's assistant, and a behavior specialist. Sam also receives several related services, including physical therapy, occupational therapy, and speech therapy. Lisa praises Sam's school-based team, declaring, "His team is amazing. We couldn't have asked for more."

Lisa reports that drafts of the IEPs are sent home in advance for her to review, and while she has input in forming goals for Sam, she jokingly states, "I don't actually have to write the IEP by myself anymore." Sam's teachers call Lisa the day before the meeting to ask her if she has any questions related to the draft, which is reviewed at the IEP meeting. Lisa and Joel are both invited to the meeting and are able to attend. "I truly feel like part of the team, where I didn't before," Lisa declares.

In his current nonpublic school environment, Sam is thriving. He is on a small dose of antianxiety medication and sees a psychologist once a week. Lisa assists her son to develop coping skills, which are reinforced at school. They practice yoga, meditation, and mindfulness together, and he asks for his own Tibetan singing bowl for the upcoming Christmas holiday. Although Sam is currently participating in school via distance learning, he still checks in the classroom behavior specialist first thing in the morning and in the afternoon. She is also available "on call" during classroom Zoom meetings, where any of the students can send her a private message and ask to go to a breakout room to debrief. Lisa calls this practice a "life saver" due to the relationship and rapport that Sam has with the behavior specialist. On occasion, Sam will continue to make self-harm and suicidal statements when he becomes angry or frustrated. Even though he has told his parents as well as school staff that he does not intend to hurt himself, Lisa understandably states, "It's hard to hear him talk like that." The connection the students have to their classroom staff has become more evident with the onset of distance learning, and Lisa states she is eternally grateful for their patience, empathy, and understanding of Sam and the other children in the class.

VANESSA

Vanessa is an Italian American bilingual woman with a nonbinary child, James, whose pronouns are they/them/theirs. James is a fifteen-year-old student in the tenth grade who is eligible for special education services under the category of autism (AUT). I was never involved in James's IEP; however, I met Vanessa through the district special education parent–teacher association (PTA), which has since evolved into the Special Education District Advisory Council (SEDAC) when James was in the sixth, seventh, and eighth grades. James attends a nonpublic school for students who receive special education services, which is paid for by the high school district. They have attended nonpublic schools since the fourth grade. During their fourth-grade year, James was suspended from school with no specific return date. At that time, Vanessa secured an attorney versed in special education law. As a result, James transitioned to a nonpublic school setting, which is on a self-contained campus with no mainstreaming opportunities, that is, special education students do not interact with their peers who do not receive special education services. Vanessa instructs preservice teachers at the university level. Both Italian and English are spoken in the home.

Prior to this dialogue, Vanessa and I had spoken to each other for about twenty minutes total, yet she immediately responded to my invite to participate in a conversation about her experiences with special education and the IEP process. We connect on one of the first days of the December rainy season, and the weather is the inevitable discussion opener.

"Every time I say 'he,' they're correcting me; my child is 'they' now."

Vanessa admits she is still struggling to use the correct pronouns for her child, who has identified as gender nonbinary since the beginning of their freshman year in high school. However, throughout our conversation, there is no indication of hesitancy, nor does she make any errors in pronouns. James, who is turning sixteen in a few months, is "virtually sleeping" through their sophomore year in high school. Vanessa relays that her child had taken a screenshot where they are sitting alert looking directly at the camera, and set that as their Zoom default photo. Vanessa shares that it took James's teachers nearly three weeks to recognize that their student is not actually participating in class. "It was extra nap time," Vanessa says with a laugh, "they are a growing teenager."

Vanessa recounts that James, as a student who receives services under AUT, has a history of the "typical obsessions that kids on the spectrum get into." There is a period of time where everything was *Doctor Who* related, and before that a much longer phase of fascination with Hot Wheels. James wants to know everything about Hot Wheels, and buys as many toy cars as their allowance allows. The cars, still in their plastic and cardboard packaging, hang on the walls in James's bedroom. Vanessa shares that for the past several years, James has been playing music with their guitar. In pre–COVID-19 times, Vanessa would drive her child to local coffee shops and shows for open mic nights. James is heavily involved in the do-it-yourself (DIY) scene in the area, has their own Bandcamp page where their songs are available for streaming and purchase, and sells cassette tapes of their music to fans through zines. They want to start their own record label, and Vanessa is currently working with James on the legal paperwork needed to create a small business. "They are my first client as a music rep," Vanessa states as she laughs.

"In retrospect, it was right there in large letters."

Vanessa admits that she and her former spouse dealt with a significant amount of denial about their child's behaviors at a young age. She shares with me that James's preschool teacher mentioned they are having a difficult time sitting still during circle time, which both parents wrote off as "silly." Even though the majority of the students in her child's class maintained a certain level of focus, Vanessa's partner "didn't want to think in that kind of direction." In other words, neither Vanessa nor James's father accepts the feedback that James's behavior differs from that of other children. James does not receive any early intervention (EI) services as a young child, and their pediatrician has no significant concerns about the child's development and growth. Vanessa refers to James as a "spirited child who was extra intense." As they enter kindergarten, James's teacher expresses concern about their "weird and different" behaviors, and encourages Vanessa and her former spouse to seek an evaluation for special education services. Vanessa stresses that the teacher utilizes humor when she relays James's behaviors, which is helpful for Vanessa in coming to terms with her child's exceptionality. Some of the behaviors include running up to the fan and lifting their shirt so air could flow underneath, removing shoes and shoelaces in the middle of class, and running up to peers and kissing them. At this time, token boards and positive reinforcement are successful in reducing the majority of their behaviors.

After much encouragement and prompting by James's kindergarten team, they are assessed and found to be eligible for special education under AUT as well as speech and language impairment (SLI). James receives pull-out support from the resource specialist (RSP), speech services in the classroom, as well as an individual aide to assist them with remaining on task for select times of the day.

From kindergarten through second grade, the services offered through the IEP enable James to keep up academically with their peers. Vanessa praises the kindness and understanding that her child's primary teachers demonstrate in providing accommodations for James. However, at the same time, James's behaviors begin to escalate at home. Having James sit and complete homework assignments becomes an increasingly difficult task. James throws books, pencils, and chairs at Vanessa and their father. Vanessa states, "I had to lower my expectations of what I asked of my child, and to be honest, it was just hard." Although Vanessa and her former spouse agree to an assessment and consent to the implementation of the IEP, the denial and grieving process of raising a child with differentiated needs continues.

"We didn't know what was going on; the school didn't either."

As James enters third grade, the curriculum and expectations become more rigorous, and the behaviors they exhibit at home cross over into the school day. In addition to throwing objects at adults, James begins eloping out of the classroom and entering other classes without permission. This behavior coincides with a staffing change of James's aide, and Vanessa shares that neither she nor her ex-partner are notified until after the switch. Vanessa shares that this was one of the first instances where she began to distrust the school team and explains that the staffing change was "hidden" from her. "Of course, it's going to affect [them]," she states.

As Vanessa explains the incident that led to James being indefinitely suspended from school, her eyes visibly well up with tears. One day in the third grade, James became frustrated after a test was taken off their desk as they walked to the back of the classroom to get some water. Their teacher refuses to return the test to James, and they respond by running out of the classroom and off school grounds. No one chases after James, but Vanessa recalls receiving a phone call from the principal who had put in a call to the police. James returns to campus approximately two hours later, escorted by two police officers, and is suspended indefinitely from school. According to California Education Code, school administrators are required to send a student's parents or guardians a letter citing a particular infraction with a set number of suspended days. Vanessa does not recall receiving this letter.

Vanessa attests to how James's principal not only violated the Education Code, he violated protections afforded to students through the IEP. When a student is suspended for ten or more school days within a year, an IEP meeting called a manifest determination (MD) must be held to determine if the student's suspension and the associated behaviors are a result of their disability. If this is the case, the IEP team is mandated to explore additional interventions, supports, and services for the student. There was no MD meeting held for James, who was not allowed to attend school for twenty-six school days while the situation was investigated.

Vanessa shares with me that she has replayed this scenario in her head hundreds of times in the seven years since it occurred. She is able to understand that her experience as a mother of a White child running from campus is significantly different from a mother of a student of color. Vanessa brings up multiple instances where young boys of color have been murdered either by police or civilians, specifically Tamir Rice, who was killed by police at the age of twelve in 2014 while playing in a public park in Cleveland, Ohio. "When the police put their hands on my child, that was it for me," Vanessa recalls, continuing to speak and cry at the same time. She pauses and declares, "As a White mom, my concerns are different. They brought my [child] back." I ask her if she needs to take a break, as this is an emotionally charged portion of our dialogue. She declines the break.

"Make a change or else!"

At this crucial point, other mothers at the district's special education PTA make Vanessa aware of the legal representation available for students who receive special education services. She and her ex-husband have no specific goals or placements in mind for their child, but they both desperately want James to feel "safe and successful at school." Vanessa feels that the district employees who facilitate the special education PTA meetings are simply "going through the motions" and "checking the box saying they gave parents an opportunity to voice their concerns." Feeling that her concerns are not going to be addressed through this venue, Vanessa and her ex retain a special education attorney, who is recommended by a fellow parent.

The attorney helps guide Vanessa and James's father with specific wording and verbiage for communication with school staff and files paperwork on their behalf to the Office of Civil Rights (OCR). She also advises them who they should speak to, and who they should refer to her office. This attorney establishes connections with several of the district administrators and makes phone calls on James's behalf. At the same time, she provides Vanessa and her ex-husband with information on nonpublic schools (NPSs) in the area that provide services and instruction to students with IEPs. Ultimately, the district offers James a free, appropriate, public education (FAPE) at an NPS that primarily works with students who exhibit behavioral challenges. This placement is highly recommended by the attorney, so James begins their fourth-grade year at a new school site.

"As the needs change, the experience at school must change."

After fourth grade, James attends three NPSs that serve a variety of students with IEPs. At the first school, which James attends from fourth through ninth grade, James begins with specialized academic instruction

(SAI), occupational therapy (OT), speech therapy, and physical therapy (PT). As they continue to make progress in these domains, James is reevaluated for eligibility for these services. By the time they enroll in high school, Vanessa recalls that James has "graduated" from all but their specialized academic instruction time. In addition, they receive both individual and group therapy, which continues to this day. Vanessa shares her concern that as behavior management and proactive responses to student behavior is the primary focus of the school, academics become less of a focus. In order to keep James up to grade-level standard instruction, Vanessa and her ex-husband pay out of pocket for a private tutor, "since [they] really [weren't] getting that at school." Despite this, Vanessa praises the teachers and staff at James's first NPS.

"We're not gonna call you unless it's something really outlandish."

During eighth grade, James begins to question their gender identity and begins requesting that people use they/them/theirs pronouns. They come out as nonbinary at the beginning of ninth grade and are subjected to bullying and harassment by several of their peers. Around this time, old behaviors, such as throwing desks and chairs, begin to manifest for the first time in several years. James's school utilizes seclusion rooms when students are perceived as being a danger to themselves or others. Vanessa explains that staff are just "sticking them in a room and leaving them there," often justifying James's seclusion as a way to prevent bullying. James begins to refuse to attend school, and their grades suffer as a result.

When Vanessa and her ex-husband receive a letter from the California Department of Education (CDE) notifying them that an investigation into allegations of bullying and harassment has been completed, she is shocked by this letter because up until this point she has been unaware of the gravity of the situation. Vanessa learns that a staff member at the school filed an anonymous complaint on James's behalf, but neither parent received a notice from the CDE of this filing. At this point, Vanessa emails the site administrators at the NPS, the special education administrators at the high school district now responsible for James's IEP, as well as the attorney they had previously retained. The district responds by immediately offering another NPS with comparable services.

James attends a second NPS through the remainder of ninth grade. They are never able to adjust to this new setting, which is more rigid than their previous school. Vanessa calls this school "extremely oppressive," noting the point sheets that James and their other peers are mandated to fill out every fifteen minutes in order to show that they can self-monitor their behavior. At this point, James is not extrinsically motivated by points, rewards, or incentives, and as a result continues to present with school refusal behaviors. In March 2020, when the COVID-19 pandemic results in full-time distance learning for the majority of students around the world, James does not log into their classes and advocates to their mother to go to another school for the rest of their high school career. Vanessa expresses her concerns to the high school district again, this time without the attorney attached to the email, and a third NPS is offered for the start of the 2020–21 school year.

"It's like graduating."

When James and Vanessa attend the intake meeting for James's new school, Vanessa reports being extremely excited about the different academic options available at the new site. James, however, takes a bit longer to adjust to their new school, until they are introduced to their new peers through a Zoom classroom. Vanessa describes her child's new friends as "artsy, loving, and caring," and she says she can hear James on the phone at night with some of their friends, laughing and carrying on conversations. Even though their social life has improved, it has been harder to get James acquainted with returning to a regular school schedule. There is a window of opportunity during the fall of 2020 when for a few weeks their school is offered via hybrid learning with in-person classes a few days a week. This ends when James's van driver contracts COVID-19 and James and their family are mandated to quarantine for two weeks and go through contact tracing. Vanessa expresses she is too scared to have James return to any type of in-person learning for the near future. She relates the dilemma she faces "that was the only unsafe thing we were doing, because it was that important." Our discussion ventures into talk of vaccines, priority lists, and when our world will return back to some type of normalcy. One of Vanessa's hopes is that James is able to have a typical high school graduation in May of 2023, to which I wholeheartedly concur.

"A Rolodex of staff members and professionals."

As James is a student who attends an NPS paid for by the school district, Vanessa interacts with many educators who have different roles in ensuring that James receives the services that they are entitled to. At the district level, for both the elementary and high school districts, there has been a program specialist assigned to James's IEP, who collaborates with the school to make sure that timelines are met and assessments are administered on schedule. Vanessa, while speaking highly of the persons who have taken on this role, explains that they have all been extremely overwhelmed and some of them have never met her child face to face. She has more frequent contact with the staff at the NPS sites, who work with James on a regular basis.

Vanessa sees a distinct contrast between the ways the public and NPSs work with parents. At all three of the NPSs James attends, the school team provides Vanessa with a draft of the paperwork in advance, and any proposed changes are outlined to her prior to the meeting. At the public school, Vanessa often felt "blindsided" when a school-based team member waited until the meeting to propose changes in services or goals that were in the IEP document. "It wasn't completely deceptive, but it kind of was." Vanessa explains, "Just tell me in advance so I have time to think about it before springing it on me in the middle of the meeting."

"Every child deserves the experiences that my child has."

Despite continued difficulties with getting James to attend all of their classes, they are flourishing at their new school. Vanessa expresses gratitude for the educators who have put her child on a trajectory to success in any field they wish to pursue. At the same time, Vanessa critiques school district funding, noting that there are not enough resources and services to meet the needs of all the students. "It's a fight for resources," she says. "It doesn't seem fair that it's an uphill battle to get what you need for your child."

Toward the end of our dialogue, she provides me with some recommendations for improving education for all students:

- Maintain smaller class sizes for all students, not just for those in more restrictive settings.
- Eliminate standardized testing and focus on more authentic and student-centered means of assessment.
- Provide an additional box on IEP paperwork for students who identify as nonbinary. Presently, the Special Education Information System (SEIS) documents still have James designated as male.
- Offer art and science classes for all students.

Specific reminders that arise out of these parent dialogues:

- It is important for all educators to understand the laws and legal guidelines that support transgender and gender-diverse students in school settings, while at the same time balancing student privacy, rights, and parent involvement in their child's education. This can be extremely challenging, especially if educators are learning as they are doing.
- In California, laws that protect transgender and gender-diverse students are:
    - California Antidiscrimination Laws in the Education Code
        - Section 220
        - Section 230
        - Section 234.1
    - Title IX of the Education Amendments Act of 1972
    - Family Educational Rights and Privacy Act (FERPA)
    - School Success and Opportunity Act (AB 1266)
    - California Healthy Youth Act (AB 329)

- In a time when sharing one's personal pronouns is more common, it is important to remember that our students may not have a fully defined understanding of their gender expression and identity. Use inviting language when engaging in a conversation where pronouns may be shared. In addition to this, a student may not be out in all environments. Let your students lead the conversation and ask before assuming. Affirming our students' identities is key to creating a safer, more inclusive campus.
- Make all students aware of counseling and other resources for transgender and gender diverse students in your community. Investigate if your city or county has a pride center or other organization that you can refer students to, as well as educate yourself on gender, identity, and expression. I'm lucky to have access to the San Mateo County Pride Center (https://sanmateopride.org/), and am honored to sit on their community advisory board.
- Of the utmost importance is that transgender and gender-diverse identity is *not* itself a qualifying condition for special education services under Section 504 or the Individuals with Disabilities Education Act (IDEA).

POST-DIALOGUE REFLECTION

My conversation with Lisa about Sam's depression and anxiety hit some very personal notes for me, specifically around the issue of mental illness. Growing up, several members of my immediate family had undiagnosed and untreated mental illness. When I first noticed signs of my own clinical depression in my early teens, I reached out for support at school and was encouraged to talk to my parents about seeking therapy. However, when I spoke with my parents, they stressed that prayer and recommitment to our Catholic faith would solve my "problems." As a result, I sought therapy on my own, using my wages from a minimum wage food service job to access sliding scale psychotherapy services at a youth LGBTQ+ center in Manhattan twice monthly after school. I have accessed therapeutic services on and off for the better part of thirty years. Ultimately, my own struggles with depression lead me to work with students coping and working through their own emotional and behavioral challenges for the first five years of my teaching career. Lisa's advocacy for her son, which includes accessing the institutional knowledge she has as a former special education teacher, brought up feelings of regret, wishing I had the same familial support system that Sam does. It is also important to note the significant contrast between the support that Lisa and Sam received in the public school system versus the care that they receive from the nonpublic school team.

After my dialogue with Vanessa was complete, I went into the IEP database to check if there was an option to correctly identify students as nonbinary. As I expected, there is an option to make this adjustment if a teacher or staff member goes one layer deeper into the system. I emailed my colleague at the high school district regarding this and gave a quick "how to" on how to make this correction. I then followed up with Vanessa and let her know to expect a change on James's records the next time she has an IEP meeting with the school district.

Vanessa retained legal counsel for James's IEP when their civil rights had been violated after an illegal indefinite suspension from school, and she reminded staff about her ability to bring legal action upon the school district when she copied the lawyer to an email after her child was bullied and secluded without cause. Her experiences with both public and nonpublic schools would have been significantly different had she not had the navigational capital to access legal representation. From my experience working with some nonpublic schools for a significant portion of my career, school districts often receive information related to student discipline and behavior days or weeks after an incident has occurred. This creates significant barriers to working with the entire team toward solutions-based collaboration. Communication prior to and between meetings can provide avenues for parents to be better informed and prepared in anticipation of any changes to their child's IEP.

When we think about diversity, we often do not take into consideration our students who identify as LGBTQIA+. In order to be truly inclusive, we must make strides toward understanding and recognizing all of the intersecting identities that our students and families bring to school, and how to ensure that all students and families are respected, represented, and heard.

Reflection Questions

- How does your school support students who exhibit challenging behaviors? What resources are in place? What else is needed?
- What are the suspension guidelines for students in your state? How have these changed over time?
- Research NPSs in your local area. What information are you able to gather from their website? How do they support the specific needs of their students?
- Describe how educators can seamlessly weave the experiences of LGBTQIA+ students into classroom lessons and activities? Look into the professional development requirements and legal obligations in your state related to transgender and gender-diverse students.
- What are the lessons learned from these two parent narratives? How are their experiences similar? How are they different?

CHAPTER 7
Judi, Aida, and Rachel

....

JUDI

Judi is a Chinese American woman with two daughters: one enrolled in a district preschool and the other currently in the fifth grade. Her elder daughter, Betsey, is eligible for special education services under the categories intellectual disability (ID) and speech and language impairment (SLI). I was part of Betsey's Individualized Education Plan (IEP) team during her second-, third-, and fourth-grade school years as the program specialist assigned to her school site. Judi and her husband, Steve, have been active members of their daughter's IEP meetings, and will request that they record the meetings so they can review the draft IEP again at home with the recording at hand. During a portion of the 2019–20 school year, Betsey's *po po* (maternal grandmother) served as a volunteer in the classroom. There was some concern on the part of the special education teacher that Po Po (all of the students and staff members addressed her as such) was inhibiting Betsey from independently completing tasks, and conveying information about the classroom back to Judi. In my conversations with the teacher on the matter, I reassure her that any observations on the part of the student's grandmother will not result in punitive action against her and suggest using this as an opportunity to build a deeper connection with Betsey's family. Po Po, while still supporting Betsey during some activities, becomes a general classroom helper, and many of the other students benefit from her guidance and reminders.

  At Betsey's last annual IEP, which was held the day before schools in California shifted to distance learning due to the COVID-19 pandemic, Judi expressed that she intended to homeschool her daughter. She continued to participate in her fourth-grade special day class activities through

Judi, Aida, and Rachel
Source: Art by Chris Holland. Reprinted with permission.

the end of the 2019–20 school year, and was withdrawn from school approximately a week into the 2020–21 school year. Both English and Mandarin are spoken in the home.

"My, how time has flown by."

I am looking forward to connecting with Judi over Zoom, as it has been several months since we last saw each other. Her daughter's IEP was the last in-person meeting I facilitated before schools went full-time distance learning due to COVID-19. Since then, my assignment has changed and I no longer work directly with the school where her daughter attends as a fifth grader. As Judi logs on, her younger daughter, now in preschool, is standing next to her, asking for help putting a straw in a juice box. I then realize that it's Thanksgiving break week, and both girls are off from school. I relay my disbelief that her younger daughter is so big, and reminisce about when she was an infant, sleeping soundly during IEP meetings.

Judi describes Betsey as a hard worker who is able to persist through difficult tasks. Betsey is eager to learn and can express her frustration through short sentences and hand gestures. According to her mother, she loves art, Legos, and puzzles. I recall how every time I walk into her classroom Betsey is always at her desk, smiling. Judi laughs and says, "She loves learning so much. She's just like a pretty happy little girl."

"So we pulled her out; we're homeschooling now."

When schools in California and around the world transition to full-time distance learning in March of 2020, school changes not just for Betsey but for millions of students. However, Judi tells me how difficult it has been at home, and that in order for Betsey to fully participate in her classes over the laptop, her mother, father, or po po needs to sit next to her throughout the day. This experience provides Judi a deeper understanding of what Betsey is learning in school and what her daughter needs in order to thrive in a classroom setting. Judi had been contemplating withdrawing Betsey from the public school system for some time, but this was "the needle that broke the camel's back." COVID-19 may have been the deciding factor in Judi's decision to have more control over her daughter's learning. Judi elaborates by saying, "If I have to sit next to her throughout the whole school day while she's on the computer, I might as well be sitting next to her and actually not be in front of the computer."

Since homeschooling began for Betsey at the beginning of this school year, Judi reports that her daughter's confidence has increased and she is more willing to speak up for her wants and needs. In addition to this, Betsey is more social. Judi explains, "There is no more screen to hide behind anymore." Betsey continues to receive speech therapy and occupational therapy, which are provided through her parents' insurance. Her sessions are conducted over Zoom, as well as in person, following COVID-19 safety protocols. Betsey's focus has increased as well, and Judi attributes this to reduced screen time. Since she is not on video calls all day, Betsey is less prone to Zoom fatigue and can sustain her attention for longer periods.

". . . and all we heard was, 'No, she's not able to do that.'"

Betsey is identified as having significant cognitive impairments from infancy, and receives early intervention (EI) services through her parent's insurance, as well as through Golden Gate Regional Center (GGRC). GGRC supports families with the transition from an Individualized Family Service Plan (IFSP) to the IEP around a child's third birthday. The school district offers a spot for Betsey in a preschool special day class (SDC) on one of their elementary school campuses. Judi emphasizes that, in addition to the special education program that Betsey qualifies for, she and her husband want Betsey to have the experience of going to school with "neurotypical kids." However, the school district provides their rationale for Betsey to remain in the segregated setting for the duration of the school day. The district, according to Judi's recollection, is hesitant to have a student with cognitive impairments participate in general education preschool, mainly for fear of overwhelming Betsey. Judi recalls that one of the teachers states that Betsey is happy in her current setting and that she has a friend in the class, the only other girl in the program. Judi goes on to question the teacher's assertion: "Is she friends with her because that's her only option, or is she friends with her because she is truly and genuinely friends with her? She didn't get the chance to try and find friends in the other classes."

Judi does not believe that the school district is affording Betsey the opportunity to spend time in the general education classroom where she can socialize with a wider range of her peers. To further illustrate her points, she uses the metaphor "testing the waters." Judi talks about how both of her daughters were initially afraid of sitting in the bathtub full of water and would only take showers. She did not expect the girls to be immediately comfortable with the full experience; instead, she eases them into the idea of a bath by first having them dip a toe in the water, then a foot, then gradually increasing the time and percent of the body that was submerged in the water. "Why can't this work for our students in school? Why are schools afraid to step into the bathtub?" she asks me. Judi believes that the school district is afraid to have Betsey fail, so they hold her back in a place where she is comfortable.

Judi's observation connects with the medical model of disability and how persons with an identified disability are perceived as limited in relation to their peers. In addition, a student's race dictates the performance expectations set forth in schools, which leads to students with IEPs consistently not meeting standards (Thorius & Tan, 2016). Judi and her family experience low expectations at an early point in Betsey's educational journey. As a result, Judi and her husband enroll Betsey in a private preschool setting that she attends after her public school day is over. This second preschool has a local reputation for inclusivity and does not deny enrollment based on a student's identified disability or need. However, since the school is private, the tuition is not attainable for many families who may see the same need for their child but do not have the financial resources, widening the equity gap between families with financial capital and those without.

"Because we had checked that box, we were refused entry."

For Betsey's second year of preschool, Judi attempts to register her daughter for the preschool classroom located on the campus of the district's Mandarin immersion school. As Mandarin is the second language spoken in the home, Judi feels strongly that her children have ties to their native language, despite all three adults living in the home speaking fluent English in addition to Mandarin. Judi would like for both of her daughters to be bilingual and stresses the benefits of comprehending multiple languages in social and work settings. Despite her efforts, Betsey's registration for the preschool class is denied on the grounds that as a student currently enrolled in a SDC, the Mandarin program does meet the specifications of the least restrictive environment (LRE) as outlined by the Individuals with Disabilities Education Act (IDEA). To put it another way, the school did not have the programs in place to support a student with Betsey's needs in the context of a dual immersion program. There were other schools in the district that could meet her academic and therapeutic needs but did not have the coveted dual immersion component.

Judi sends multiple emails to the site principal, as well as the assistant superintendent of student services and the director of special education. She does not receive a response that meets her satisfaction and ultimately decides to drop the matter because "if they're not even gonna want her in the first place, if I send her there, they're just gonna find a reason to kick her out. So, I dropped it."

Judi states that she is now "always on my guard" in interactions with school staff, but in particular site- and district-level administrators. She questions, "Are we adversaries? Are we really working together? I don't really know." When parents lose their trust in the educational system, there must be an effort made within the school to regain and repair the trust in the interest of the student and their needs (Herrera et al., 2020; Freedman, 2017).

"Oh man, we could have done better."

Judi shares her feelings of disappointment in her ability to fully comprehend the special education process from the onset of her family's journey. Both Judi and her husband work in a profession where measurable goals are part of their daily work lives, but she states that understanding what constitutes an effective or realistic goal for Betsey has been difficult. Judi admits that "all this trust in the experts to make up the right goals is perhaps the hardest part" of the IEP process, because she is used to having a sense of control over the goal-making process in her career. She says that learning what to look for in a goal and what questions to ask came with the experience of sitting in multiple IEP meetings for Betsey over a number of years, as well as comparing IEP goals with other parents of students in the special day class. Judi believes that IEPs are written "for the convenience of the school district, and in a way that the teacher can act on it in the classroom," and states that the parent perspective is not taken into consideration when developing the document. Here, Judi clearly articulates the interrogation of who the IEP is written *by* and *for*, and how her lived experience and perspective was disregarded in favor of professionals (Herrera et al., 2020).

As further evidence of who controls the IEP process, Judi shares that she does not receive a draft of the IEP paperwork or assessment reports prior to the meeting without having to request the documents. Not having the paperwork before the meeting, Judi asserts, makes it difficult for parents to be prepared and participate in the decision-making process. Even after making the request for drafts, it is only in the past two years that she receives a comprehensive draft from Betsey's teacher prior to the IEP meeting. Judi states that there are several times when she feels unprepared during the meeting and says, "Okay, I guess we'll just take that for now, that sounds about right," only to second-guess her choices when she gets home. "I'm not sure if that's what she really needs," Judi admits. Since Betsey started first grade, Judi has been audio recording the IEP meetings and plays it back while she reviews the paperwork at home prior to consenting to anything. "I never sign anything at the meeting, except attendance," says Judi. "I need more time and a quiet space to make sure I know I am doing the right thing."

"I had to keep pushing, again and again."

Throughout Betsey's time in the district, communication with staff is inconsistent. Judi reports that there has been a significant amount of staff turnover during Betsey's elementary school career, which impedes her daughter's progress. Betsey requires an extended period of time before she is comfortable with new adults. Before Betsey trusts a teacher or therapist, she is extremely quiet and does not participate to her full potential. Judi praises the efforts of Betsey's speech-language pathologist (SLP) over the past few years. This SLP has been the most consistent member of Betsey's IEP team, and often supports new staff in introducing them to Judi, and reviewing Betsey's historical IEP files. Despite this, Judi reiterates that she often has to ask questions multiple times and make requests several times before receiving a response to a query. She clarifies, "I'm always the proactive one," and laments that it is rare for a staff member to initiate a conversation about Betsey's progress. In order to have as much face-to-face contact with staff as possible, Judi drops Betsey off at the classroom door a few moments before the bell rings in the morning so she has a chance to chat with the teacher. She shares pickup responsibilities with her mother, Po Po. The multigenerational family structure provides parents additional opportunities to work extended hours, as Judi and her husband do, while having a relative as the primary caretaker (McGinley & Alexander, 2017; Tutwiler, 2017).

When I ask her what she would like or expect Betsey's teachers to share with her, Judi states that she would like to hear about what her daughter did during the school day, as well as any concerns that the teacher or staff members may have about Betsey's progress. She believes that school staff are apprehensive about communicating with parents in a way that could be misconstrued, or that they may not have the adequate knowledge with which to provide parents the appropriate information. "You're always hoping for the miracle, even though you know there's no magic pill to make all of [Betsey's] challenges go away," Judi laments. "We're just looking for someone to hear us out and tell us we aren't completely crazy." In other words, Judi is seeking partnership from school staff, as well as validation that her concerns and worries are heard. When school teams do not provide this essential piece of support to parents, communication and collaboration can be perceived as disingenuous and inauthentic. Ocasio-Stoutenburg and Harry (2021) illustrate this perfectly when they state that parents "need(ed) respect and equity for their person" (p. 191).

"It's almost like a joke to us parents."

Judi exudes frustration when the topic of occupational therapy (OT) in the school district comes up. Out of all the services providers under the umbrella of special education, OT has experienced the greatest turnover and shortage of staff. Judi reports that there have been several school years where Betsey has multiple occupational therapists assigned to work with her, as well as extended periods of time where OT services are not occurring because of a staff vacancy. She elaborates by saying that "most of the [occupational therapists] have been really sweet girls, but they are here one day and gone the next," identifying that while staff intent may be positive, the inconsistency is the issue at hand. In her conversation with other parents, Judi reveals that several parents have begun to outright decline OT services altogether in order to maintain a consistent routine for their child. For Betsey, Judi advocates that OT services be provided as a consultation to the special day class teacher in lieu of direct services with her daughter. Judi values the time that Betsey spends in the classroom, and wants her to generalize the skills she requires in class as opposed to practicing them in a self-contained environment such as the occupational therapist's office.

"This is what we do every day and this is what she does."

As Betsey transitions into second grade, her IEP team recommends that she switch classes. Up until this point, Betsey attends a special day class for students considered to have moderate to severe disabilities. Judi, as well as several other members of the IEP team, notice that Betsey's independent abilities far exceed those of the other students in her class. As a result, the district offers Betsey a spot in a classroom for students considered to have mild to moderate disabilities. Judi explains that Betsey is now one of the "lower kids in the class" and expresses frustration because she does not believe that the classroom staff push Betsey academically as much as she would like. She explains:

> What I was really hoping for is like, "We think Betsey can really do this, and this is how we're gonna get there, and this is what Betsey's gotta do to get there." And so I felt like that was lacking. But everyone's always generally been responsive, with a little pushing, and if we had specific questions, they were happy to answer them. But again, in general, I think because everyone is busy, it did require us to be proactive.

Once again, Judi demonstrates that she has often had to be the initiator of conversations about her daughter's progress. Much like her view on the role of the occupational therapists, she sees the good intention of the staff but also recognizes that limitations of a structural and systemic nature may be the underlying reasons for the difficulty in communicating with staff. "They only have so much time in the day," she elaborates. "I get it."

"She was just a visitor, just passing through."

The school that Betsey attends for grades two through four prides itself on the opportunities it creates for mainstreaming and inclusion for students with IEPs. It is one of the district "model" schools for inclusionary practices; however, Judi recalls that she always feels she needs to advocate for Betsey to spend time in the general education classroom. Even after this, the times identified as optimal for mainstreaming were all electives, or "soft subjects," as Judi calls them. When Judi asks if Betsey can attend a general education math class and work on math with one of the SDC paraeducators, the option of a kindergarten class is offered. "That's not what I want for her. How could they even suggest sending her to a room with five-year-olds?" Judi understands that Betsey's academic abilities are not at the same level as her peers in a general education class but wants Betsey to have time to socialize with a wide range of children her own age. She rejects the idea of having Betsey go to kindergarten. Betsey has a legal right to be in a classroom with her peers. This exclusion is reified in public schools and society because "the status quo works well for the dominant group, students from non-dominant groups experience the imbalance of power and are required to either fit into the existing structures or to risk being relegated to alternative or 'special' classrooms or schools" (Ferri & Connor, 2006, p. 130).

For the three years that she attends this elementary school, Betsey participates in music, art, physical education, and some science classes with students in her current grade level. According to Judi, however, Betsey is never perceived as a true member of the classroom community. "I don't think the teachers ever thought of Betsey as being one of their students," Judi recounts. Instead of having a desk of her own, Betsey squeezes into a space with some other students, often toward the back of the room. By denying Betsey her own relegated space in the classroom, she is invisibilized and not seen as an equal. Judi relays that "it wasn't really in her best interest the way it was set up. It was what was convenient for the teacher." To put it another way, Judi is asking for both creativity and acceptance on the part of the classroom teacher, instead of having Betsey fit into the mold of the class structure and layout. This ties back to the proactive/reactive paradigm that has been illustrated several times throughout her narrative thus far.

"There is a finite timeline for our kids."

Over the years, Judi raises her concerns not only to the IEP team but to special education leadership as well. She always maintains a positive relationship with district level staff, but grows weary of the messaging that she receives. Instead of addressing the issues at hand, Judi feels that the focus remains on forward thinking and mapping. When I asked her how she feels about this attempt at proactive planning on part of district staff, she says,

> Well, it was good to know we would have these conversations and acknowledge the problems and acknowledge like, "This is what would have been great." And we would have these grand ideas where it's like a plan, but I'm like, but that doesn't help me. That doesn't help these sets of kids who are in these upper grades now. It's sort of like, not wasted, but it's sort of wasted, right? They have not been able to get the full impact of what you were hoping or expecting to get.

The frustration that district-level planning will not directly benefit her daughter is what sets Judi on a path exploring options for homeschooling her daughter, as well as having her mother, Betsey's po po, begin to volunteer in the classroom in the middle of fourth grade. At first, Po Po unintentionally acts as Betsey's individual aide and provides her with an overload of prompting and support that results in the teacher calling an IEP meeting to express her concerns. After the IEP, Judi explains to her mother that she would like Betsey to work more independently and to support her only if needed. Another IEP follows in the winter of Betsey's fourth-grade year, and Judi asks for a reduced class schedule for Betsey so she can work with her daughter at home on specific tasks related to her IEP goals. This schedule is put in place right before the shelter-in-place of March 2020 due to COVID-19, and shortly after Judi removes Betsey from the public school altogether.

"I feel like it would be really challenging."

Judi does not know if she will return Betsey to the public school system after the COVID-19 pandemic. She does, however, provide several suggestions that she thinks would be important for schools and districts to enact in order to prevent or mitigate some of the barriers she has experienced in her journey with her daughter.

- "Soft academic" classes such as art, music, and physical education are default for having students in segregated classes mainstream with general education peers.
- Schools should establish buddy/peer friend and lunch bunch group opportunities to foster genuine friendships and social situations for all students. Judi stresses how important this is for her and Betsey, "so that students with IEPs know they belong right away, and so that students without IEPs can learn compassion and empathy, and that all staff can come to understand that all kids deserve those opportunities." This shifts the current paradigm, which mainly focuses on the benefits for students with IEPs. Students who do not receive IEP services also greatly benefit from playing and collaborating with peers with a wide range of abilities and needs.

My dialogue with Judi ends with an extremely profound statement where she recognizes her privilege. She says, "We always had to ask to be included, and not everyone knows to ask. Parents shouldn't have to ask." I agree with her wholeheartedly, and we close with a promise to keep in touch, regardless if she returns Betsey to the district.

AIDA

Aida is a Pakistani woman with one child. Her eleven-year-old son is currently enrolled as a sixth grader in a private school in the same city as the school district. Previously, Hassan was a student in the district from kindergarten through fifth grade. He is eligible for special education services under the categories autism (AUT) and speech and language impairment (SLI). I have worked with Aida throughout my tenure with the district, as her son changed schools and settings. Hassan received support from the resource specialist (RSP), as well as support from a special circumstance instructional assistance (SCIA), also known as a 1:1 aide, from kindergarten through third grade. For fourth grade, he transitioned to a special day class (SDC), and his 1:1 aide services were discontinued. Aida works for a nonprofit organization geared toward lobbying major publishing houses to print children's books that celebrate diverse cultures and traditions. She has presented at conferences and workshops in the area geared toward culturally relevant pedagogies. Her husband is a mathematical engineer who works for a technology company.

"Like all of us, he is still a work in progress."

I always love having the opportunity to chat with Aida, and this afternoon is no exception. Aida texts me a few moments before our scheduled start time to let me know she's running a few minutes late after assisting Hassan with a reading assignment. In actuality, she is right on time, although still apologizing profusely. Hassan is doing "relatively well" with distance learning, and is independent in logging into his classes and keeping up with his assigned work. Aida describes her son as a mellow young man who follows directions. It is only within the past two years that he initiates others in conversation; now Aida calls him "quite chatty." Hassan loves geography, and his favorite subjects in school are math, science, and social studies. Aida clarifies that anything that is based in fact, or has a "hard" answer, is easy for Hassan to comprehend and soak in. Aida recognizes that Hassan faces challenges in communicating his knowledge and understanding to others. She relays that Hassan "knows more than he lets on because I think language is a barrier . . . but he surprises us all the time with things that knows. Every day there is something new that just astonishes me about my son."

Although he was considered a "late bloomer" in terms of his expressive language development, Hassan carries a "dog-eared" book of idioms with him at all times. He often utilizes the idioms he learns in conversation, much to the surprise of his conversational partner. In addition to this, Hassan loves vocabulary, word puzzles, crosswords, and the game show *Wheel of Fortune*. Aida shares that some of her friends have begun to question if Hassan has been "cured" of his autism, but she shakes her head and calls this "such a simplistic viewpoint" on the autism spectrum disorder. She acknowledges that Hassan continues to grow and make progress, but there are still several areas where he has challenges. Reading comprehension is a particular area that Hassan has difficulty with, even though he is able to read nonfiction textbooks and other information from websites. Literature, with the exception of science fiction, "are the bane of his existence," because there are no clear answers to be found.

"It's been a little bit of a journey."

Aida shares with me that Hassan receives a medical diagnosis of autism around eighteen months of age and, soon after, is enrolled in an early intervention (EI) preschool. Each class at the preschool serves six to eight children, with teachers and educational staff who are extremely warm and caring. Although Hassan cries a lot at first, he becomes accustomed to the routine and structure that his classroom provides. Each child is taught how to zip and unbutton clothing, hang up jackets and backpacks, sit in a group circle and their individual seats. Aida states that Hassan greatly benefits from the repetition of learning how to "be" at school, and that he is fortunate to have received his diagnosis at such an early age. She observes other children who started after they turned two to have a more difficult time picking up routines. Hassan begins applied behavior analysis (ABA) therapy shortly after his second birthday.

Hassan is enrolled in a private preschool for one year and then enrolls in a district inclusion preschool class when he is four years old. This class, which enrolls twelve students, is structured similarly to a kindergarten class to best prepare students for that transition. At the transition IEP from preschool to kindergarten, the IEP team recommends a general education kindergarten class for Hassan, with support from the resource specialist and district autism team. Although the kindergarten class has twenty students, Aida and her husband believe that Hassan will be able to "handle it." The preschool teacher provides the incoming kindergarten teacher with strategies on how to best work with Hassan, and Aida feels "completely satisfied" with her son's move to kindergarten.

"Things would get . . . overwhelming."

During the summer before Hassan's kindergarten year, his projected kindergarten teacher resigns for personal reasons, and a newly credentialed teacher is hired to replace her. The institutional knowledge on successful support strategies that his preschool teacher passed onto the kindergarten teacher is also lost, as she, too, leaves the district. Aida reports how quickly it became apparent that there are "too many students and too much noise" for Hassan to manage his emotions. As a result, he has several meltdowns during the day, which necessitate a quiet space for him to decompress, as well as walks outside the classroom to cool down. Aida describes her son as "the kind of kid that implodes." His behavior does not affect the learning of his peers, but he shuts down and ceases all verbal communication. Hassan's teacher asks Aida if she can volunteer in the classroom to assist with her son, and Aida gladly obliges. Aida states that her full-day volunteer position lasts three months, during which time she proactively takes data on specific times of day and particular activities or environments that trigger Hassan's meltdowns. Aida utilizes this data at his annual IEP in kindergarten to request an assessment to determine eligibility for an SCIA, or a 1:1 aide. In addition to the aide, Aida also requests assessments for SLP and OT. While the school-based IEP team is conducting the evaluations, the site administrator reallocates a paraprofessional aide to assist Hassan for the last two hours of the day. Aida's observational data indicates that Hassan requires extra support during recess, and late morning academics through dismissal at 12:30 p.m. An IEP is held before Hassan's transition to first grade. At this meeting, he is found eligible for speech and occupational therapy services, as well as a 1:1 aide for the entirety of the school day. A binder of supports is developed by the district-based autism team, with input from Aida, to support Hassan as well as his new teacher and aide.

"I have to advocate for my son."

In first grade, Hassan's school day is extended to 2:45 p.m. Despite the efforts and work that went into the development of the resource binder, it becomes apparent that neither Hassan's new teacher nor the paraprofessional assigned to him are utilizing identified resources and/or accommodations to support his sensory and emotional needs. Hassan continues to have at least two meltdowns a day, and the principal notifies Aida that the teacher "doesn't have the time to cater to his every need when she has other students in the class." Aida is visibly agitated as she relays this encounter to me and says, "Sometimes teachers have a particular way of doing things and they don't want to necessarily change that, even if it's for a child who needs some accommodations. As a parent, this can be incredibly disheartening."

Aida becomes further disheartened as neither the teacher nor the principal returns her emails in a timely manner. Generally, teachers are asked to return or acknowledge a parent email within one to two working days; Aida states that many emails went unacknowledged or replied to after a week. Because she is receiving so little communication about her son's behaviors and progress, she starts visiting the school campus during lunchtime. Aida checks in with Hassan's paraprofessional who is providing support to him and his peers on the playground. Hassan's teacher and principal reprimand Aida for speaking with the paraprofessional without their consent, and this creates an additional rift in the relationship between her and the school team. Aida rolls her eyes as she justifies her actions, "They weren't giving me a response, and I needed to get my answers. I'd do it again if I had to."

Through her check-ins with the paraprofessional, Aida finds out that the paraprofessional is being pulled from the classroom at the beginning and end of the school day to perform crossing guard duty, two times where the previous year's assessment determined that Hassan requires her support the most. Aida requests several IEP meetings during Hassan's first-grade year to state her concerns about the inconsistencies in support, communication, and the lack of academic progress. Aida feels that her concerns are not validated or considered. She is left with the impression that the teacher and principal only meet with her because the law requires them. Aida feels that the body language and tone of voice that these two staff members display present as if they are thinking, "Ooh, this parent is angry and this parent is ranting, so let them rant, but we're not going to change anything. Let her go on and on and on, we're not going to change one thing."

For the last IEP of the year, which serves as Hassan's annual IEP, Aida brings a staff member from the music therapy organization that serves Hassan outside of school. Aida states that this therapist served as a "support system" and advocate for both her and Hassan, and "helped me get my voice heard." The music therapist makes remarks throughout the meeting when she senses that the general education teacher or the principal are not listening to Aida, or are disengaged from the process. Surprisingly, at the end of the meeting, the principal apologizes to Aida and commits to actively listening to her moving forward. Aida confides, "This meant a lot to me, because I knew we were going to have to continue working together." The only comment that Aida makes about Hassan's second-grade year is that it was "significantly better" than first grade.

"The new IEP team, they just got it right away."

At Hassan's annual IEP toward the end of his second-grade year, the team discusses the possibility of a change of placement to a special day class on another school campus. The RSP at Hassan's school contacts me, the program specialist assigned to that elementary school. I meet Aida for the first time, and I show her two different classrooms on other school campuses. A third classroom has a full enrollment and thus is not an option for Hassan for third grade. Ultimately, the team decides to postpone the change of placement until the following school year, with the hopes that the third classroom will have an open spot for Hassan.

Aida's concerns about increased rigor in academics lead her to push for a change of placement as Hassan enters fourth grade. The entire team agrees that the special day class, which serves up to twelve students with IEPs, is a good fit for Hassan. As the classroom is staffed with several paraprofessionals, the school team proposes discontinuing Hassan's individual aide services from his IEP. Aida agrees with this decision because she wants Hassan to develop his independence.

Hassan is in a class with the same teacher for his fourth- and fifth-grade years. Aida praises this teacher who takes the time to review his IEP before the school year begins and calls Aida to ask clarifying questions. "That meant a lot," Aida shares.

> I never had any concerns when he was in that class, he was happy and so were we. They knew exactly what they were talking about; they knew exactly the ways in which to intervene in different situations. It was a perfect combination of experience, optimism, and positive attitude that was a recipe for success.

Aida is describing what all students need and deserve in order to grow academically, socially, and emotionally. While we both agree that a change of school should not be necessary to find an environment where Hassan can flourish and thrive, she is thankful that he was given a new opportunity for the last two years of elementary school. It is during these two years that she sees the significant progress in Hassan's ability to express himself verbally, and his burgeoning love of academics. The growth he makes in the fourth and fifth grades is also what leads to her pause in enrolling him in the public middle school for sixth grade.

"Middle school, that was a huge hesitation for us."

At the beginning of the 2020–21 school year, amid the COVID-19 global pandemic, Hassan's parents decide to place their son in a small private school that specializes in teaching students on the autism spectrum in lieu of having him attend a special day class at the middle school closest to their home. Aida states that she has concerns about class size in middle school, which can rise up to fifteen students in the special day class, as well as reports of bullying of students in self-contained classrooms. She does not want Hassan to "get lost in the shuffle of it all," and this is the impetus for the family's decision to withdraw him from public school. Aida states she does not intend to seek reimbursement from the school district, clarifying that "I know they could do a good enough job of working with Hassan, but I want the best for him, and I know that can't be done in a public school setting."

According to Aida, switching to private school has not eliminated barriers to Hassan's success. Aida notes that Hassan is performing above most of the peers in his classes, and she has had to reach out to his teachers several times for requests to extend his learning, either by offering him a deeper dive into the content or an accelerated pace. She says she "feels like I'm knocking constantly at their virtual door saying, 'What are you doing now? What are you doing now?'" Even with tuition payments, Aida is having to advocate for her son and proactively seek out extra support in order for him to receive instruction at his ability level. To this end, Aida states that, in her experience, public school teachers have consistently communicated more effectively than the teachers at Hassan's current private school. In addition to this, she states that public school IEPs are generally more detailed and data driven than the documents the private school has provided her up to this point. She further clarifies by saying that "I always felt that working with the IEP teams was always great because we were all just trying to move forward to supporting my son." Aida states that she feels "disappointed and let down" that the private school has not followed through with what was promised before enrolling Hassan. She expresses some regret in withdrawing him from the public school system and has not made a decision yet as to if she will reenroll him for the seventh grade.

"I haven't found that magical place yet."

When I ask Aida what Hassan's ideal learning environment would look like, she first states that it would "absolutely" be on a public school campus. Both Aida and her husband believe in the strength and power of public education, and want to be part of what Aida calls "the possibility of the great equalizer." Aida envisions this perfect classroom would have a class size of less than ten and be supportive of students' social-emotional needs, have sensory breaks embedded throughout the day, and focus on academics, with high expectations for all students. Up to this point, Aida shares that she has only found this over the past two years in Hassan's fourth- and fifth-grade classroom and hopes that the "just right balance" exists out there as he gets older.

"Cultural humility is so important."

Aida states that there is often a cultural mismatch in the expectations that school-based team members have for both students and families. We have previously discussed how the Western expectation that children make eye contact with a speaker is contradictory to the norms of many other cultures. Aida plainly states, "We're taught not to look at our elders in the face." In addition to this, Aida recognizes that even adults are conditioned to be deferential to authority figures, which would include teachers and school administrators:

> Most immigrant cultures are taught to be very respectful towards authorities, to be very respectful towards teachers, you don't question them. But I feel like you have to advocate for your child, and if some of that means questioning what's going on, then you have to question what's going on. You can't just take everything that's given to you as a be-all and end-all. You have to understand why they're saying what they're saying, and if that doesn't work for you, you have to be able to communicate that to the team to say why this is an issue. And I feel like most other parents just give up. Like they just . . . they won't go into this conversation. They will just take their kid out of the school. Or they will just move to a different location so that he could be in a different space. Or find a more immigrant-friendly sort of place or something like that. But don't give up, I haven't given up. Sometimes you have to be brave enough to confront the problem you see.

Aida is not advocating for immigrant parents to simply assimilate and take on a more "Western" confrontational style of communication. Rather, she has come to understand that parents must view themselves as equal members on the IEP team, at the same level as school and district staff. She encourages parents to stay in the conversation, ask questions, and not "give up."

RACHEL

Rachel is a Black woman with one child. Her thirteen-year-old daughter, Emily, is currently enrolled as an eighth grader in a private school in a neighboring city. Previously, Emily was a student in the district from kindergarten through fifth grade. Emily was assessed twice by the school district and was found to be ineligible for special education services despite an independent evaluation with a diagnosis of dyslexia. I was referred to speak with Rachel by another parent I engaged in dialogue with for this research. Her private school has an intervention program specifically for students with dyslexia. Rachel works in the office of the school that Emily attends, and she co-parents Emily with her ex-husband.

Despite not qualifying for an IEP, I feel it is important to include Rachel's story in my research. Rachel considers her child to have a learning disability (LD). She has received a medical diagnosis from a doctor at Stanford, and she receives support for dyslexia in school. In addition, as the sole Black parent participant in my study, it is essential for her experiences and perspective to be documented (McCarthy Foubert, 2022). Finally, when I was referred to Rachel by the other parent, I was not aware that Emily had never received IEP services from the school district, only that she had dyslexia. Considering that Rachel committed an hour out of her day to share her story, I feel a strong moral obligation to honor and respect her time and effort.

"She's a sports gal."

Rachel is just getting home from work and informs me that she will have to pause our dialogue at some point for dinner delivery. She said she wasn't able to cook tonight because she was extremely tired. I express my gratitude and double-check to see if she has the energy to chat this evening. After she replies in the affirmative, she begins to tell me about Emily.

An athletic teenager, Emily excels at any sport she tries. Currently, she is on a soccer team, and swims regularly. She recently expressed interest in playing rugby, which came as a surprise to Rachel. "Who knew?" she responds with a laugh. "It's kind of a bougie sport, but okay." Emily also loves theater and was looking forward to a trip to New York City to see *Hamilton* for her thirteenth birthday in June of 2020, but this was postponed indefinitely due to the COVID-19 pandemic. Her love of theater crosses over into a newfound interest in books. Rachel explains that Emily used to actively dislike reading but has become obsessed with reading plays and books about stage productions. Emily has asked for gift cards to Amazon and Barnes and Noble for Christmas this year so she can purchase books tied to this interest. Emily is also a major sneakerhead. Rachel exclaims that her daughter has about thirty pairs of sneakers at each of her parents' houses, and that she knows how to find good deals on deadstock Nikes, her favorite brand.

"It will come together eventually."

Rachel's concerns with Emily's academic abilities, specifically in reading, start when her daughter is in preschool. Even though her teachers report that Emily is "incredibly bright," she struggles with letter identification and sounds. During the intake process for kindergarten, the school nurse advises Rachel to take Emily to see an optometrist, as she believes that Emily's difficulties with her letters are related to her vision. However, glasses do not resolve Emily's issues with reading. Rachel reports that from kindergarten through second grade, Emily demonstrates extremely advanced verbal communication skills and vocabulary, but her decoding and reading comprehension are well below the expected benchmarks for her grade level. When she expresses her concerns about Emily's progress in reading, each of her teachers for these three years downplays the situation, stating, "Sometimes they don't come together at the same time." Rachel shares with me that her frustration grew with each passing year as she continues to see her daughter grapple with increasing expectations and rigor. "Were my concerns disregarded because I'm Black and the teachers are White? Probably. But that's just how the system works. They aren't going to stop me from raising those concerns about my baby though."

"It was tears every night."

Rachel defines "the breaking point" when Emily enters third grade. Using a frequently utilized phrase in education, she explains, "This is when kids switch from learning to read to reading to learn." Emily has not mastered the learning to read portion of the statement, and this leads to her breaking down sobbing as she attempts to complete her homework at night. Her grades begin to slip even as her effort increases. Rachel reports that Emily begins to bite her fingernails and has difficulties sleeping, sometimes wetting the bed. Rachel shakes her head and sighs, visibly agitated at the memory of this dark time in her daughter's young life. Meanwhile, Emily's peers are "doing cool things in school, and she's falling behind." When Rachel approaches Emily's third-grade teacher and the school counselor, she states that they were, to me, saying that they knew that there was an issue, but they couldn't put a name to it, because if they say that there was an issue, then that means that they had to put an effort behind it, basically. And so that was frustrating because it was like the teacher was really listening to me and she was understanding, but she wasn't really giving me much more than, "Yeah, I see what you're saying, and I agree, but not really much," and she wasn't really giving me much to help me or my daughter.

Rachel believes that Emily's teacher agreed with her concerns, but there was no follow-through to discuss specific strategies, accommodations, or interventions. This lack of proactiveness on the part of school staff leads Rachel to take action.

"Enough was enough."

As her frustrations with the inaction on the part of school staff grow, Rachel begins to learn more about learning differences, and specifically about dyslexia. She states that this begins with a simple Google search, which brings her to Understood (www.understood.org). With this new information in hand, Rachel makes a verbal request to the counselor for assessment for special education services. After a staff member, whose position she does not recall, observes Emily in class and conducts a file review, the school-based team determines that an assessment is not needed and that Emily is "doing fine." Rachel vehemently disagrees with this decision and appears in person to the district office to make a second request for an assessment. It is there that she is asked to provide her request in writing so that the district can recognize it as a formal request. She is provided a "stack" of forms to complete.

When the assessment is complete, a meeting is held to discuss the results of Emily's testing and to determine eligibility for special education services. The school-based IEP team states that Emily does not meet the criteria for a student with a specific learning disability (SLD). Rachel states that she felt the assessment was inadequate, and did not specifically address her concerns around dyslexia. "It didn't seem like it was enough," she says. "I walked out of that meeting more frustrated than when I walked in."

"Bumping our heads, and learning on our own."

Returning to Understood's website, Rachel finds additional information about testing for dyslexia in her county. She says, "Okay, well, maybe I'll go get her tested," and pays out of pocket for private testing. After the agency that specializes in dyslexia completes the testing, Rachel requests a meeting with Emily's school and brings representatives from the agency to explain the results of their assessments in detail. The private agency's testing states that Emily has dyslexia and outlines a plan for remediation and intervention so that she can become successful in school. At this meeting, Rachel requests that the school district reassess her daughter, who is now in fourth grade, "and come up with a plan and how to address her needs."

"It may have been more of a resource thing."

The school district reassesses Emily and utilizes the private assessment data in their report when considering her eligibility for special education. She discloses to me that the team determined a seventeen-point discrepancy between Emily's performance and her measured ability. I asked her what batteries or measurements the district used, as students who identify as Black cannot be given IQ tests, per the *Larry P.* decision of 1979 (Woods & Graves, 2021). Rachel says she recalls hearing the school psychologist reference this, but recalls hearing about a seventeen-point discrepancy regardless. The district does not recommend an IEP for Emily, and instead offers a 504 plan. Rachel learns that a 504 plan is not overseen by the special education department and while it provides students with accommodations in order to access the curriculum, students do not receive services such as resource (RSP) support. Rachel believes that the school team was hesitant to offer an IEP because of the stigma attached to receiving a label of special education, particularly for a Black student. She recounts that they stated that the 504 plan provides more flexibility but did not go into specifics.

The offer of a 504 plan is not perceived as an acceptable solution by Rachel. She recalls sitting in the meeting reviewing the results of the assessment and seeing Emily's classroom teacher shaking her head as the school psychologist reads her report. Rachel further explains that

> her teacher's hands were tied and that she knew there was an issue, but she couldn't just flat out say "I think she had dyslexia,"

because if they say there's an issue then they have to put money behind the resources to remedy the issue.

In addition to the district's reluctance to allocate resources, none of the school staff specifically mentions dyslexia by name, and Rachel believes that this is because "if that word ever tumbled out of their mouths that would have tumbled us right into an IEP." In other words, members of the team intentionally refrained from using key terminology that might have triggered an enactment of an IEP and eligibility for special education services. For Rachel, this is a betrayal of trust that she continues to carry with her. At this point, Rachel decides to stop fighting for an IEP for Emily and instead pays for her daughter to attend a private program after school, which assists with remediating some of her struggles with reading and teaches her strategies to mitigate some of the difficulties she has as a result of her dyslexia. When Emily completes this program at the end of her fifth-grade year, Rachel makes the decision to withdraw her from the public school system and registers her at a private Catholic school.

"It was just a seamless transition."

Rachel explains that there are two main factors that influence her decision to place Emily in private school. First, the Catholic school has significantly smaller class sizes; there are forty total students in Emily's grade level divided into three separate classrooms. Second, this school comes highly recommended by the dyslexia program that Emily attends, and has an established working relationship with the team. Prior to Emily's first day, her new school meets with the team from the dyslexia agency and they develop a plan with accommodations and supports that are specific to Emily's unique needs. Rachel refers to this as "their own version of an IEP," and the way that she describes the meeting is extremely similar in nature to a public school IEP meeting. It is a collaborative effort, as Rachel describes, with all team members sitting together, figuring out how to serve Emily. However, Rachel does state that the school-based members of the team do the majority of the talking, with her and Emily's father "taking it all in, but they are absolutely open to our input. It's not like they shut us down or anything like that."

At this private school, Emily's plan is adjusted at least once a year depending on her changing needs as she ages and progresses. Currently, Emily has tests read to her and extended time on assignments when she advocates for herself. Rachel reports that her daughter is "thriving" in her current setting. When I ask what her plans are for Emily when she reaches high school next year, she states that Emily will be returning to public school because tuition at private high schools in the area are two to three times the cost of private elementary school. When Rachel shares the plan for next year with Emily, she is delighted to hear that Emily is excited by the prospect of attending her local public high school, along with some of her friends. "That meant the world that she feels like she will be okay," Rachel says as she smiles widely. "For me, that's the most important thing out of all of this."

Important Reminders That Arise out of These Parent Dialogues

- Be aware of the particular means of communication that exist between the school, district, and families. Many of the teachers that I have worked with recently like the Remind (https://www.remind.com/) app, because a teacher's personal cell phone number stays private and messages can be translated into more than ninety languages. Schools and districts are using platforms such as Parent Square (https://www.parentsquare.com/) since it's app-based as well as web-browser-based. Translations for messages are available in more than one hundred languages.
- Think about the ways that your school and district currently engage parents and families. Who are the families on your school site council (SSC), PTA (parent–teacher association), or PTO (parent–teacher organization)? Are they the same families? For site leaders, make sure that you are utilizing all of your district's resources to engage a wide variety of families, including representation on your ELAC (English Learner Advisory Committee), which is mandatory in the state of California.
- All staff, be they general education or special education, must understand the procedures and timelines that protect students and families related to requests for assessment. A parent request for assessment must be taken seriously and responded to within fifteen days of receipt. It's essential that school team members know who to pass requests along to; many times, it's the school psychologist, while in other settings those requests go through a program specialist or special education administrator.

POSTDIALOGUE REFLECTION

Judi has the resources with which to provide her daughter with the academic support that she requires, as well as the related services such as speech and OT through her insurance. At the same time, I think of other parents who may be experiencing similar situations who do not have the resources that Judi and her husband have at their disposal. The fact that Judi was willing to share her story after she had made the decision to homeschool Betsey is a valuable reminder to me of my intentions behind this work.

School-based IEP members need to understand that they are not the only members of the team with expertise in children. I recently attended a conference where one of the panels was focused on "reclaiming" the label of expertise for school-based staff. The presenter stressed that education staff proudly call themselves experts in order to take ownership of the knowledge they hold. This did not sit well with me, and I typed a comment in the chat that educators also need to recognize the expertise and familiar knowledge of parents and caregivers. Sadly, this comment was disregarded by the panelist, and I left the panel disillusioned. At the same time, it reinforced the *why* for this research. Elevating myself to the role of "expert" where I can present these findings can shift the narrative to where parents' knowledge and expertise is elevated to the same level as school-based team members.

When, within the first few minutes of our conversation, Rachel discloses that her daughter has never qualified for an IEP in public school, despite being formally assessed two times, I debate whether to continue the conversation or to disqualify her from this study based on my predetermined set of requirements. Reflecting on this now, I am glad I trusted my instinct to continue the dialogue, because learning about Emily's struggles in school and the barriers that Rachel encountered significantly influences my understanding that denial of services can be as discriminatory as placing a student in a segregated special education environment. Denying support and services to a Black family who continuously advocates for their daughter is exclusionary, and this narrative provides a firsthand account of the ways in which the system neglects students and families of color.

Reflection Questions

- How can schools welcome and include nonnuclear families into the community? Think of some traditional school events that assume the presence of a mother and a father, bake sales, father/daughter

dances). How can teachers and leaders expand or adjust norms to reflect inclusivity?
- Judi reports her daughter's confidence, focus, and self-advocacy have increased since she has begun homeschooling. What structures or norms need to be in place in your classroom for those three characteristics to be nurtured and developed?
- How can our nonverbal communication impact our interactions with others? What are some ways that we can demonstrate that we are interested and engaged with what is being discussed? Conversely, what are some ways that may demonstrate we are not interested or inattentive to the conversation? How would that impact our relationship with families?
- After reviewing the definition of least restrictive environment, what is your understanding of it and how is it applied in your classroom(s)? How is sending Betsey to a kindergarten classroom for math instruction not compliant with the law?
- Aida openly shared her vision of a perfect classroom and Judi shares her suggestions to prevent or mitigate barriers she and her daughter experienced. Visualize a walk-through of your future or current classroom, or a class at your school site, through the eyes of one of your students' parents. Without judgment, what do you notice about the physical and nonphysical space available to your students? What could you redesign to assure each student has space and place for access and opportunity for success and safety? What are your nonnegotiables for this space?
- What are the lessons learned from each of these three parent narratives? How are their experiences similar? How are they different?

CHAPTER 8

Possibilities

....

A SUMMARY OF THE NARRATIVE INQUIRY

Throughout these eleven dialogues, each parent describes the inherent tension that exists between the desired outcomes of parents and families, and the outcomes typically offered by school and district staff. While parents and families want what is *best* for their children, schools are only mandated to provide what is *appropriate* or *adequate*. Teachers and other education staff, while they may promise (and even intend) the *best* are constrained by the resources available to them, thus creating a conflict that goes beyond semantic understanding. As voiced by Betsey during our dialogue, this tension leaves parents wondering, "Are we really working together?" I felt the power of her question and was so impacted by it that I used her words in the title of my doctoral dissertation (Vogel-Campbell, 2021).

The dialogue narratives reveal several facets of the often fraught and/or tense relationships existing among parents and the special education educators who are called to serve and support their children. Convenience of the educators, disregard for parent perspectives, parents feeling forced to serve as advocates, and a desire for assets-based learning and collective problem-solving are the common themes that emerge across the parent dialogues.

Parents consistently cited examples of how student accommodations are offered based on what was convenient for the teacher, the program, the school and/or the district, not necessarily the student. School-based members of the IEP teams present parents with proposals that often reify the status quo with minimal adjustments. Educators' unwillingness to change: the physical environment of the classroom to include students with disabilities (Judi, Tomas); lesson pacing and structure (Aida); and behavioral intervention strategies (James and Eiko) left parents questioning the intentions of the teachers who work with their children. Each of the eleven collaborators speaks to the difficulty in getting their child evaluated for services, and then having those services enacted on a consistent basis. Even with the backing and support of case managers and school personnel, this undertaking is arduous; Gloria and Tony illustrate this when they state, "We knew he needed something else, the teacher said he needed something else, but the district still said no." Legally mandated timelines can support a slowed down process that is in opposition to the urgency that parents feel when advocating for assistance for their children. Judi describes the window of opportunity for her daughter as "finite," and Leticia shares that "timelines don't really mean much when they are ignored." Lack of communication also contributes to diminished opportunities for students with identified needs that necessitate special education services. All of the limitations and constraints that schools and districts subject parents and families to result in diminished chances for meaningful participation in the IEP process.

Throughout our dialogues, parents shared numerous instances of how their perspectives on the optimal learning conditions for their children are disregarded. For instance, parents typically want their students to have opportunities to interact with their peers in general education settings, yet Judi's request is ignored, while Gloria and Tony, Aida, and Roger must "push" to get some mainstream time for their children. In addition to exclusion from general education activities, Gloria, Tony, Rachel, and Judi find they are unable to secure their students' access to specialized programs. There are also several instances where students were required to move school sites in order to enroll in an identified program. However, there is little evidence that school-based staff comprehend the significance and implications of this change for parents and students. Schools must move toward a deeper discussion of the sense of urgency that parents experience, as well as ways in which school staff can work toward creating empathetic environments so that parent concerns are valued and validated.

All of the parents in this research identify the need for parents to act as advocates for their children. Parents describe being pushed to serve as advocates. When parents sense a disharmony with the IEP team, any implicit trust is broken. For instance, Roger cites staff "not having done their homework" when they fail to read prior assessments before contacting him as a breach of trust. Along the same lines, Emily is hesitant to place trust in school-based IEP members who "don't have the time to talk," and who "interrupt you at every opportunity." Rachel states that "enough was enough," and several parents utilize the navigational capital they possess as educators to open doors of opportunity. Other parents seek the services of advocates and attorneys to assist them in maneuvering through the special education process. Despite possession of professional status and resources, there are instances when even the most privileged parents are too tired to fight. After unsuccessfully trying to get his daughter assessed for special education, Roger says, "Forget it," and waits until after the family moves to a different state to restart the process. Aida embodies the perseverance of parents in adverse situations when she states, "But don't give up, I haven't given up. Sometimes you have to be brave enough to confront the problem you see."

Finally, the last common thread woven throughout the parent dialogues is a desire for assets-based thinking and collective problem-solving. It is bitterly ironic that not only is this what parents overwhelmingly want, this approach is commonly accepted as best practice in every classroom, school, and district. Educators may be familiar with buzzwords such as growth mindset (Dweck, 2008) but may not be incorporating the ideas and tenets of cultural humility (Tervalon & Murray-Garcia, 1998) or community cultural wealth (Yosso, 2005) in their interactions with students and families. Parents yearn for school environments that incorporate and honor their familial knowledge, as well as recognize the aspirations they have for their children.

In order to better understand how parent narratives might inform practice, I first examine the findings through the theoretical frames of community cultural wealth and disability studies. With these frameworks in mind, I then critically examine educator focus group participants' responses to excerpts from the parent narratives. This critical examination illuminates special educators' resignation to current practices that conflict with their underlying beliefs as to how parents should be engaged as partners. Finally, recognizing the harm inflicted by current practices, I explore possibilities for growth and systemic change.

FINDINGS AS THEY RELATE TO THE THEORETICAL FRAMEWORKS

As stated previously, I choose to utilize two theoretical frameworks to guide my research: community cultural wealth (CCW) and disability studies in education (DSE). Both CCW and DSE are frameworks that stress the importance of an intersectional approach to research and inquiry. In order to fully meet the call set forth by these critical frames, I feel it is essential to cross-pollinate them (Waitoller & Thorious, 2016) and interweave them throughout the work.

COMMUNITY CULTURAL WEALTH

Yosso's (2005) framework of community cultural wealth consists of six interconnected forms of capital: aspirational, linguistic, familial, social, navigational, and resistant. Community cultural wealth centers and honors the experiential knowledge that students and families bring to school that is often disregarded by White hegemonic systems and structures. I often hear teachers and other educational professionals speaking to a need for educators to help parents realize their knowledge and worth, as well as that of their children. These educator statements are premised on an assumption that families do not recognize their own capital, knowledge, and assets. As evidenced by the parent dialogues presented in the past few chapters, this is a false assumption that is dangerous and damaging to the teacher–parent relationship. It is up to educators to recognize and understand the gifts and knowledge that students, parents, and families bring to the proverbial table. Judi exemplifies this sentiment when she states, "We're just looking for someone to hear us out and listen to us for once."

Aspirational Capital

Each parent who collaborated in dialogues speaks to the aspirations they have for their child. Tomas, while he expects to be Isaiah's primary caretaker for the remainder of his life, wishes for his son to be "happy and healthy." Vanessa is optimistic for James's music career and the innovative and creative ways they market their songs and music. The aspirational capital that Gloria and Tony hold for their son, Jeremy, to attend college is similar to that of Aida and her son, Hassan. Parents have hopes and dreams for their children and wish for them to live fulfilling lives (Gregg et al., 2012; Larios & Zetlin, 2012).

Linguistic Capital

Connected to parents' aspirations is the desire for children to have language skills in their home language. Judi wishes for her daughter, Betsey, to learn Mandarin. James and Eiko place a high value on Nao having an understanding of one or both of his home languages (Spanish and Japanese). By allowing Nao to choose which language he learns, James and Eiko reinforce the power and knowledge of linguistic capital (Burciaga & Erbstein, 2013; DeNicolo et al., 2015).

Familial Capital

Yosso (2005) prompts us to expand our notions of the definition of family beyond the nuclear family unit ideal perpetuated by White American culture. In this study, Judi refers to Betsey's po po, her maternal grandmother, as "something like a third parent." The COVID-19 pandemic resulted in Tomas's adult children and their partners moving back to the family home, and everyone contributes in some way to Isaiah's care. This is an embodiment of familial capital, the intergenerational knowledge, customs, and traditions nurtured by the extended community.

Social Capital

Networking with other parents is a common thread throughout several of the dialogues with parents (Judi, Emily, Vanessa, and Gloria and Tony). These network interactions provide parents with additional knowledge on services and resources (Fernández & Paredes Scribner, 2018) and strengthen their understanding of the parents' legitimate role in their child's IEP. References to advocates and lawyers' information, as well as clarifications on rules and procedures that are too often ineffectively explained by school and district staff are passed along by word of mouth, parent to parent, family to family.

Navigational Capital

It is important to recognize that each parent has a different set of resources and privileges that may either ease or inhibit their ability to navigate through systems not structured with parents' needs in mind, especially families of color (Bejarano & Valverde, 2013). Many of the parents who participated in dialogue have direct contact with the school system through their careers: general education classroom teacher (Roger), university level educator (Vanessa), classified staff (Rachel), former special education teacher (Lisa), educational organization presenter (Aida), paraeducator (Eiko), and school administrator (James). For families without this insider knowledge, leveraging their social and resistant capital enhances their ability to maneuver through complex situations, such as special education and the IEP. Learning from the experiences and knowledge of their friends and community, and employing their resiliency, supports parents' preparedness to ask questions, challenge inaccuracies, and question assumptions made about their families or children.

Resistant Capital

Finally, all of the parents who collaborated in dialogue utilize various forms of resistant capital, the ways in which traditionally minoritized peoples subvert and survive in oppressive situations that are rooted in defiance and opposition to injustice (Burciaga & Erbstein, 2013). As unfortunately indicated throughout the parent narrative, students who have an identified disability, as well as their parents, have been minoritized and othered by society as a whole and the public school system in particular. The clearest example of resistant capital narrated in the parent dialogues is Tomas's negotiation of IEP services for Isaiah. Tomas, who primarily uses Spanish to communicate during IEP meetings, describes how he enters an IEP meeting with "high bids" for service minutes that his son should receive. He states,

> If I go into a meeting with ninety minutes of speech as an ideal, and they offer sixty, I can counter them and try to get seventy-five. I never expect to get the full ninety, but if I set the bar high, it can't be lowered that much.

While also utilizing navigational capital, Tomas challenges and pushes back against preconceived notions and expectations of how parents, particularly second language speakers, are expected to participate and behave in IEP meetings.

DISABILITY STUDIES IN EDUCATION

The second framework I utilize is disability studies in education (DSE), which focuses on the concept of disability within social and cultural contexts. Ferguson and Nussbaum (2012) defined clear objectives for DSE that I incorporate into my research. The study of disability must be social, foundational, interdisciplinary, participatory, and values-based.

The study of disability must be social.

Disability studies in education seeks to challenge the notion of disability as perpetuated by the medical model, which views disability as an ailment in need of rehabilitation and remediation, and results in the perception of persons with disabilities as damaged, less than, and not worthy of the same benefits/treatment/education as those without disabilities. Instead of adjusting environments and classrooms to meet the needs of all learners, schooling under the medical model of disability segregates students with disabilities in a variety of settings. In this study, we see the segregation of students in the resource room (Marcus, Ryan, Isabel, and Nao), special day classes (Betsey, Faith, Isaiah, Jeremy, and Hassan) and more restrictive settings such as nonpublic schools (James, Sam) and residential facilities (Baglieri & Knopf, 2004). Weber (2013) states that parents may believe that a smaller and exclusionary setting is in the best interest for their child, while not taking into account the harmful effects of isolating them from the majority of other students their age. Not only does this segregation pathologize the students and their unique learning needs (Annamma, 2017), in some cases, it criminalizes the students and their needs (Annamma et al., 2013). Vanessa recounts a chilling example of how the police were called after James left campus, and they were returned to school restrained by law enforcement officers.

The study of disability must be foundational.

Individuals and students without disabilities are implicitly privileged over their peers with an identified disability. It is important to understand who benefits from the labeling and othering of students with disabilities, as this creates a disabled/abled dichotomy that upholds the status quo. Judi, when discussing how Betsey participates in the general education mainstream classroom, uses the analogy of how Betsey is treated as a visitor passing through the class. Judi's statement—"I don't think the teachers ever thought of Betsey as being one of their students"—illustrates the feeling of *otherness* and exclusion that many students and parents experience. Capper (2018), when describing structural functional epistemology, relays that "whether at the district or school level, students labeled with disabilities are viewed as someone else's responsibility—that someone else is responsible for "those kids" (p. 45). Tomas, like all parents in this study, calls into question this lack of accountability. When describing his son's current program, he reports, "It's not designed for kids like him." While the medical model of disability and structural functional epistemology place an onus to change on the individual student instead of the system, disability studies in education calls for shifts at the core of structures and processes.

The study of disability must be interdisciplinary.

We must consider a variety of identities when working with students and their families: race, disability, class, gender, sexuality, and documented status being a few. Roger, as a gay, White, adoptive father of two Black children with disabilities has a different perspective and experience than a White father with biological children. "Yeah, we got some stares the first day I walked my two kids into the office, and believe me, those stares went into overdrive on awards night when my husband joined me," he shares with a laugh. Vanessa, who spoke to her child's coming out as nonbinary, and the bullying they were subjected to as a result, laments, "They were blamed for the bullying that they endured because of who they are, and that's just not acceptable. I'd like to assume that it's because the staff lack an understanding of gender identity. I hope so." Annamma et al. (2013) remind us of the responsibility educators have to recognize the multiple identities of our students, and I put forward that this extends to their families as well.

The study of disability must be participatory.

Each of the parents who engaged in dialogue stressed the importance of participation in the IEP meeting. To varying degrees, all experienced situations where they were included, but more frequently the narrative of exclusion is dominant. Vanessa recounts that several times she noticed special education staff "checking the box saying they gave parents an opportunity to voice their concerns" when in actuality she had not been asked this question. "Oh, if I had been asked, it definitely would have been a no," was her response when I asked her what she would have said if given the opportunity. Voulgarides (2018) as well as Wolfe and Duran (2013) found similar situations in their research. Conversely, Rachel describes the way her daughter's intervention team at her current private school is constantly "taking it all in, but they are absolutely open to our input. It's not like they shut us down or anything like that." One striking thing is that none of the parents reported their child consistently participating in their own IEP, an idea at the core of the participatory nature of DSE (Danforth, 2006; Connor et al., 2008).

The study of disability must be values based.

While the medical model remains systemically pervasive, disability studies in education strives to confront the status quo and provide possibilities that promote equity and acceptance. Special education services are provided through a legal compliance model, as opposed to what is best for students and families. While special education laws were initially intended to protect the rights of students and parents, they perpetuated the use of the medical model of disability. The complexity of the laws stifles creativity and innovation on the part of school-based staff and districts in providing services and programs to students. I return to an impactful statement by Judi where she shares her philosophy on public schooling "so that students with IEPs know they belong right away, and so that students without IEPs can learn compassion and empathy, and that all staff can come to understand that all kids deserve those opportunities."

Every parent expresses a desire for the school-based IEP team to view their child in a positive light, highlighting what they *can* do as well as what they are "currently struggling with." Leticia voices this collective desire for inclusion and understanding.

Leticia elaborates on her statement, "Well, maybe she'll improve her reading so we can then say she can read at grade level. I'm never going to say my daughter can't do something." By intentionally not saying *can't*, this views the learning challenges her daughter grapples with as temporary, as opposed to permanently affixed to her. Values-based and assets-based thinking will be examined at length when we examine implications and possibilities that arise as a result of this research.

VIEWING THEMES THROUGH THE LENS OF EDUCATORS

In order to maintain a space in the research where the parent narratives were the sole perspective under consideration, I stated in the previous chapter that findings related to the educator focus groups would be analyzed and reviewed here. Once the eleven parent dialogues were completed, I conducted two focus groups with special education district office staff. At the time of initial recruitment for the focus groups, there were eleven district staff members working in the special education department, not including myself. Of the eleven potential participants, nine agreed to participate and returned the consent form. To ensure that each participant would have an adequate opportunity to share during the one-hour allotted time, two focus groups were scheduled with randomly selected participants. The first focus group consisted of five members while the second consisted of four.

I selected four quotes from parent narratives with the intention of eliciting conversation around the following prompts: How might we (special education teams) consider

- the ways we can learn from parents about their child's assets, strengths, and interests?
- the ways in which we engage families about a child's learning differences?
- the ways in which we initially contact families?
- the ways in which we share the assessment process?
- the ways in which we model and support ongoing communication?
- the ways in which we facilitate understanding of the special education paperwork?
- the expectations that parents have about their child's special education services?
- the roles that parents play in the designing and monitoring of their child's educational program?

Utilizing the four themes identified in the parent narratives via deductive coding methods, I coded the transcripts after the focus group conversation. Again, these four themes are: convenience of educators/school/district, (dis)regard of parent perspectives, the parent as advocate, and a desire for assets-based thinking and collective problem-solving. With this in mind, we now turn to the theme of convenience, and how attachment to the status quo stifles the individualization required to effectively implement student IEPs.

CONVENIENCE OF EDUCATOR/SCHOOL/DISTRICT

The theme of convenience, that decisions are made based on what works best for the teacher, school, or district, mirrors the organizational theory dilemmas investigated by Capper (2018), in that "the goal of structural functionalism remains efficiency, not equity. Thus, from a structural functional epistemology, equity or social justice are not considered—implicitly or explicitly" (p. 41). Staff that participate in the focus group acknowledge the dissonance between their personal beliefs and their work in a system that consistently disenfranchises students and parents. While one of the participants observes, "I feel like we're not making decisions based on students' needs," another responds, "I don't know if it's even possible for significant positive change, we have too many students." In the quest for efficiency, "corners are cut to save time" and these cut corners include not completing paperwork on time, and copying and pasting reports using a template. Echoing the concerns of several of the parent collaborators, one staff member shares that some staff do what is easiest for them, not necessarily what is best for their students:

> Here's my curriculum, this is what I teach, and this is just how the IEP is gonna go. I've never heard a teacher say that, but that's the messaging that I think parents hear. This is what the teacher is teaching, and if you don't get it, you're gonna be moved to this teacher who teaches a little lower. I get stomachaches when I have to sit in some of these meetings.

This underlying frame is distressing, because sustaining the status quo will not result in change but, rather, will only lead to the further stagnation of possibilities for our students and families.

(DIS)REGARD OF PARENT PERSPECTIVES

There was a consensus among the staff focus group participants that parent perspectives and experiences are generally disregarded by the IEP team. One staff member asserts, "I don't really see a respect for our children and the way that they learn, and I don't really see a lot of empathy either, for what the parents are going through. I think it's a real issue." Another staff member stipulates, "It's that kind of implicit bias or just that blind spot we have coming from our context and not considering that there might be another context, another truth, another reality." Implicit bias and a failure to consider parents' experiences might be among the root causes of the disconnect that exists between parents and the school. Two participants spoke to the power of nonverbal language and cues, and admitted tendencies to not recognize or even ignore parents who are visibly uncomfortable or appear confused in meetings. "I'd like to think that it's just ignorance and that folks aren't deliberately ignoring when they see a parent doesn't understand," one staff member confides to the group.

This dehumanizing of parents in the IEP meeting aligns with the work of Zetlin and Curic (2014), who stress the need for empathetic relationships among IEP team members and families. One of the staff participants summarizes one aspect of this need for caring and authentic communication with parents. She emphasizes that "if there's one thing that you learn to do and do well, it's tell parents the truth and tell it with compassion and empathy . . . but make sure they understand what you're telling them." Educators must make a concerted effort to ensure that they understand what parents are sharing about their children.

THE PARENT AS ADVOCATE

Overall, staff believe that parents feel the urgency to become advocates for their children after they are dismissed and denied by either medical or educational professionals. In addition to this, when professional knowledge is lacking, parents are driven to educate themselves. A participant remarks that most of the parents who question the system are White and middle class:

> One of the things I love most is when a parent comes in ready to question what the school-based team is saying. But I also know that not all parents have the resources and understand that they can do that. It's mostly White parents and parents who are at least upper middle class.

The parents who collaborated on this research are a representative sample of the diversity of families in our district by race (Black, Latino, Asian, White), as well as socioeconomic status. While there is no quantitative data available to support or refute the staff member's assumption, the qualitative narratives of the parents presented here provide us with valuable insight on how families from a variety of backgrounds respond to advocate for their children. Despite this, some parents (Judi, Roger, Emily) spoke of "giving up the fight" in some areas of the IEP. A staff member reflects on how the parent voice is extinguished:

> It's not surprising, and it's really kind of sad that after hearing "no, no, no" several times, year after year, that a parent will stop asking. But that's not their fault, that's our fault for failing to do our due diligence.

Once again, recognizing that the school system often refuses to hear parent concerns is a starting point for shifting mental models and mindset and enacting change (Kania et al., 2018).

DESIRE FOR ASSETS-BASED THINKING AND COLLECTIVE PROBLEM-SOLVING

The final theme expressed in the parent dialogues is a collective desire to move toward assets-based thinking and collaborative problem-solving in special education, especially during/through the IEP process. This shift in practices requires educators to listen more closely to parents. One of the staff participants highlights the importance of honoring and utilizing parent knowledge when she states, "Parents know their kids really well and they've been through this process, so they've gone through teacher after teacher, and they know what works and what doesn't to a big extent."

The participants were hesitant to offer suggestions to move toward an assets-based approach. At first, the virtual meeting room is silent for a few moments. Unsure as to how to gauge the reasons for this pause, I prompt the group to offer suggestions based on the parent excerpts. Still, there is a hesitancy. Ultimately, I decide to move the conversation along and not to place the participants in a situation where they feel uncomfortable. However, this awkward silence makes me wonder *why* professionals freeze when I ask them to think outside the box. The other focus group provides several strategies and steps that could be taken to facilitate a mind shift to assets-based thinking. One staff member suggests a practice done in a previous district, which was "rolling narratives/Google Drive" for each child with pertinent information so new teachers and service providers can see and contribute to it year after year. Another recommendation is weekly or biweekly check-ins with parents outside of the IEP process through a phone call, Zoom/Google Meet, or even a house visit (post-COVID).

Reflecting on parent narratives is an essential task in order to answer the research questions with a participatory calling. Despite the good intentions of educators and staff, there remains an inherent tension in the relationship between families and schools in relation to the education of students with IEPs. Although these relationships are sometimes fraught with dissonance, I recognize the potentials and possibilities for growth and progress. I carry the experiences of parents and the intentions of special educators with me as I move into implications with a hope that committed special education teams might consider new possibilities.

SO . . . WHAT COMES NEXT?

Possibilities

In lieu of the more commonly used word *recommendations*, I intentionally use *possibilities*. *Recommendations* has a finite connotation that is somewhat problematic when considering the need for a paradigm shift. Access and engagement in the IEP process is not an issue based on a linear problem that can be solved with one solution. It involves, as Kania et al. (2018) describe, "shifting the conditions that are holding the problem in place" (p. 3). Hanson and Lynch (2004) frame the conclusion of their work by stressing the possibilities for growth, development, and change. Ultimately, the term *possibilities* is based in a more inclusive, assets-based, collective problem-solving approach, which harkens to the tenets of community cultural wealth, disability studies in education, action research, and the themes identified from parent dialogues.

Two of the parents, Judi and Roger, provide me with specific suggestions for the following section. I give my collaborators credit for their contributions. I begin my description of the possibilities for change by considering what should be the closest connection to the student, that is a collaboration among teacher/case managers and parents (or primary caregivers).

At every level in the special education process, a true collaborative partnership with parents must be intentionally cultivated and maintained (Kalyanpur & Harry, 2012). These partnerships must acknowledge pedagogical, social, and cultural practices that are valued and maintained in the home (Pacino & Warren, 2022; Ishimaru, 2020; Mapp & Kuttner, 2013). We must consider the possibilities for a more inclusive partnership at every level from teacher/case manager, site IEP team, site administrators, special education departments, school boards and labor unions, school districts, county offices of education/SELPAs, and the state department of education.

Case Managers

Roger provides some suggestions for case managers that he feels would demystify the IEP for parents. First, sending drafts of the IEP home in advance, rather than by request, should become a common practice in order for parents to have an opportunity to read the draft and bring questions to the meeting. He also encourages case managers to reach out to families before the IEP, and to ask parents how and to what extent they want information presented in the meeting. While keeping IEP meetings virtual at parent request after students have returned to in-person learning post–COVID-19 may not be a viable option for all, it is one that Roger feels should be offered for parents who work a distance from school.

In order to create a space where parents feel welcome, teachers and case managers can shift toward a more personal tone in their interactions with parents. While special education professionals have an obligation to adhere to specific wording during portions of the IEP meeting, conversations and dialogue with parents can veer toward sounding scripted. Eiko recalls, "Sometimes the teacher had to look at the paper before starting to talk to me," meaning that staff didn't have the necessary information needed to engage in a meaningful discussion. This is similar to Roger's plea for staff to read prior assessments and reports before asking parents redundant questions. Ultimately, this is a time-consuming task for educators and staff to undertake, but it moves practice away from staff convenience toward what works best for parents. In this way, when a parent asks, "Are we really working together?" staff have evidence that significant efforts are being made to answer with a definitive "Yes."

IEP Teams

As the case manager adjusts their practice in communicating with parents, this should be accompanied by a shift in the way that members of the IEP team interact with parents. Larios and Zetlin (2022) stress that "if we want our parents to be true participants in their child's IEP meeting, then we must embrace the style of communication that they are most comfortable with" (p. 18). School-based members of the IEP team should implement ways of incorporating visual aids into their discussions with all parents. In addition to this, educators and other special education professionals need to be conscious of the usage of jargon in their conversations with family members. When educators use acronyms, it furthers the informational divide between team members and denies parents access to information they need in order to make informed decisions. Providing full names of agencies, laws, and services, in lieu of acronyms, makes content accessible for parents and families who may or may not possess extensive background knowledge on the topic. In order to model this behavior, an acronym glossary is provided in appendix B. While IEP meetings are generally held on school grounds, the conference room or space used for the IEP meeting should be entered by all participants at the same time, and parents should be given priority as to their seating preference. Not only does this create a welcoming environment but it also sets families at ease when they have the agency to occupy the space that they feel most comfortable in. Finally, Roger brought up the idea of an anonymous survey post-IEP asking parents to rate their satisfaction and understanding of their child's IEP meeting. He feels that this can be used as an accountability tool for teachers and team members in their continued work with families.

Site Administrators

Judi shares that she would like to see schools establish buddy/peer friend and lunch bunch group opportunities to foster genuine friendships and social situations for all students. This will require support and planning on the part of the site principal or administrator, as well as coordination with a school counselor or psychologist to facilitate groups. Site administrators should also ensure that their conference rooms are a comfortable temperature, with uniform chairs for all participants. Have tissues, hand sanitizer, and water on hand. If site budget allows, invest in a circular conference table so that all participants have an equal physical position in the room. In this way, there is no head of the table, which is generally occupied by the administrator. Equipping the conference room with a whiteboard and a screen so documents can be casted for participants to view is also helpful for teams when reviewing assessments and planning.

Special Education Departments

Roger advocates for a more concerted outreach effort on part of the special education department in order to inform parents about SEDAC (Special Education District Advisory Council) meetings. He also recommends that a portion of the special education website could be dedicated to connecting families with outside community resources and organizations. Parent education nights on breaking down the IEP process for both new and existing families whose children receive special education services was also mentioned.

Recruiting and retaining special educators who speak a language other than English is also highly needed in a district where more than a dozen languages are spoken (EdData District Profile, 2023). Gloria and Tony felt welcome when their son's teacher was able to communicate with them in Tagalog. When a teacher requires interpretation, they often have to seek out a staff member or district representative who has limited knowledge of the program or the child.

Hiring bilingual classified staff, such as paraeducators, can also strengthen relationships between schools and families. Relationships are truly the way to transform a system that can lead to long-term impact (Kania et al., 2018).

Special education departments must make a concerted effort to reduce the number of students currently enrolled in segregated classrooms and schools, and work with educational services departments to ensure that students with IEPs are provided the same opportunities and level of high-quality education that students without disabilities receive (Weber, 2013). To this end, there should be increased opportunities for special education staff to gain experience with grade-level curriculum, and share their knowledge of differentiated instruction (DI) and universal design for learning (UDL) techniques with their general education colleagues. This pushes against the ideology of "somebody else's students" embedded within the structural functionalism epistemology (Capper, 2018).

School Boards and Labor Unions

Judi expresses strong support for classes such as art, music, and physical education to be inclusive of all students. She refers to these classes as "soft academics," and stresses that a student in a special day class should not have to wait until their IEP to have minutes adjusted in order to participate in these enriching school activities. This shift toward greater inclusion will involve collaboration between the district and labor unions in negotiating contracts around language and class size and/or will involve the provision of additional teachers and support staff to accommodate the change in numbers.

School Districts

Change enacted at a school-site level is supported by similar shifts throughout the district. Fullan (2007) provides guidance for enacting change in organizations, which "means creating a culture (not just a structure) of change" (p. 44). Part of this change involves being able to critically examine current practices and being intentional about which new ideas to incorporate on a consistent basis. Mental models and habits of thought pose the greatest challenge to implementing change (Kania et al., 2018). Without a shift in mindset, changes in policy, practices, and resources will be ineffective. District and site-based leadership are tasked with ensuring that emancipatory change is fully implemented with fidelity. School districts must also commit to reducing the amount of litigation with families by actively participating in the Facilitated Individualized Education Plan (FIEP), as well as Alternative Dispute Resolution (ADR), which is a more humanizing approach to resolving conflict.

County Office of Education/SELPAs

The "Notice of Procedural Safeguards" outlines the rights granted to parents and guardians of students who qualify for an IEP. This document is offered to parents at the beginning of each meeting in the language of their preference. I selected three SELPA websites based in Northern California to gauge the ease of accessing the documents and what translations were readily available for viewing. San Francisco Unified School District (2023) housed English, Spanish, and Chinese versions of the document under a "Resources for Families" tab I could navigate to in less than one minute. San Francisco also provided a link to the SELPA Administrators of California website (2023), which houses documents in thirty-five languages. The San Mateo County Office of Education (2023) provided links to eighteen documents under a "Parent and Community" tab that I found within three minutes of searching the site. Santa Clara County Office of Education (2023) linked to a Google Drive folder with thirty-two documents. This search took about five minutes to complete and necessitated a return to my search engine and performing a specific query: "Santa Clara SELPA Procedural Safeguards." Table 8.1 provides a comprehensive list of all available translations.

TABLE 8.1. "Notice of Procedural Safeguards" and Most Recent Translations

Language	Last Update
Chinese-simplified, Chinese-traditional, English, Spanish, Tagalog, Ukrainian, Vietnamese	2022
Armenian	2018
Arabic, Bengali, Burmese, Farsi, French, German, Gujarati, Hebrew, Hindi, Ilocano, Italian, Japanese, Kannada, Khmer, Korean, Marathi, Pashto, Polish, Portuguese, Punjabi, Russian, Samoan, Somali, Tamil, Telugu, Thai, Tigrinya, Turkish, Urdu	2016
Hmong	2009

Source: Special Education Local Planning Areas (SELPA) Administrators of California (https://selpa.info/info/parents-as-partners).

As a minimal baseline for more equitable services to students and their families, the County Office of Education and SELPAs should disseminate these documents to their colleagues statewide, as well as to the CDE so that all districts have access to translations for their families.

State Department of Education

While a call to standardize a process for special education may seem counterintuitive, there are scores of IEP paperwork templates used in the state of California. All of these templates align with the various elements required in an IEP, but the differences in both formatting and wording are confusing for parents as well as special education staff. I recall working with an experienced special education case manager who had over a decade of experience in Southern California who compared learning the new way of doing paperwork to learning a different dialect of a language. Providing parents with consistent IEP paperwork across the state is one step toward facilitating participation. Not having to relearn the format of the documentation gives parents the ability to focus on the content of the IEP.

In addition to providing/creating/retooling family-friendly templates, there are several student information databases currently in use in the state of California for storage and maintenance of IEPs that require immediate revision/attention/reconciliation. The two largest of these databases are SEIS, which is maintained by the San Joaquin County Office of Education, and SIRAS, managed by a private company in Santa Barbara County. SEIS and SIRAS are not compatible, meaning if a student moves from a district that utilizes SIRAS to one that utilizes SEIS, the incoming teacher must input the entirety of the last IEP into the new database, which leaves room for considerable human error and takes time away from direct service to students as well as their families. It would be advisable to implement one program across the state for more continuity; currently SEIS serves more than 80 percent of the state's Special Education Local Planning Areas (CodeStack, 2020). Roger also envisions that a parent portal could be added to SEIS so that families have an opportunity to view their child's current and historical IEPs, as well as progress reports. "Imagine all the paper that could be saved if a family just wants to go digital!" he exclaimed. "Save some trees if you can!"

Implications of the Study

Districts and schools are mandated by law to provide means of accessibility for culturally and linguistically diverse families. Oftentimes this legal mandate is viewed as an additional element that needs to be "checked off" in order to ensure compliance with state and federal requirements. When educators default to a compliance mindset, conversations about equitable outcomes for all students, as well as the ethical responsibility to work toward repaying the educational debt (Ladson-Billings, 2006) owed to students of color, are limited.

Just as schools have traditionally placed the knowledge of teachers over the knowledge of parents and caregivers, the existing literature positions some knowledge over others. Many participants in the IEP process have limited representation in the research as it exists today: fathers, extended family members, various service providers (speech and language pathologists, occupational therapists), classified school staff (paraeducators, interpreters), and community-based stakeholders (family advocates and attorneys, CBO members). There is also a lack of research on participation for families with students who have moderate to severe disabilities. A comprehensive examination of the perspectives of these individuals will expand our base of knowledge, and value knowledge that has been left out of previous studies. The intention of this research, which ultimately intends to bring together a collective of parents' voices in action research, is one step in the direction of inclusivity.

Moving Forward by Consistently Centering Families

I hesitate to use the word *conclusion*, and thus ultimately choose to utilize *moving forward*, as this study is an important initial step in the work toward centering the perspectives and narratives of families. My intention is to continue to dedicate myself to this work and, ultimately, to pass the baton to other teachers and administrators so they can work in collaborative partnership with families. In order for this to occur with consistency and fidelity, a drastic and radical shift is needed. This shift must focus on creating equitable opportunities for the diverse communities that school districts serve in order for the special education system to work for *all* students and families. We must heed the call put forth by Martínez-Álvarez (2020), when she states the need for schools to foster spaces where disability is viewed as an asset in the same vein as bilingualism and biculturalism. Schools need to move beyond compliance and construct an emancipatory reality to better support families and children. Parent voice must be the starting point in each interaction between educators and families in order to recognize the assets and knowledge that each unique family carries with them. Educators must challenge their own preconceived notions of how they expect parents to contribute to their child's IEP. This involves a critical examination of current practices, reflecting on procedures that decenter familial involvement, and altering norms to accommodate the experiences and perspectives of *all* team members. When the school-based team acknowledges the significance of parental involvement, the narrative changes from that of depersonalization and conflict to authentic collaboration, as evidenced by Lisa's praise for her child's team. She exclaims, "It's phenomenal; I can't say enough good things. His team is amazing. We couldn't have asked for more. I truly feel like part of the team, where I didn't before."

I want this to be every parent's experience, regardless of race, gender, sexual identity, socioeconomic status, documented status, language preference, or any of the multiple identities they live on a daily basis. It is our obligation to respect these identities, recognize where they intersect, and engage the funds of knowledge that parents and families contribute to their child's education.

Appendix A
Methodology

In order to understand the experiences of families and educators, the knowledge centered in the research must come from the parents and educators themselves. As hooks (1994) so eloquently states: "To engage in dialogue is one of the simplest ways we can begin as teachers, scholars, and critical thinkers to cross boundaries, the barriers that may or may not be erected by race, gender, class, professional standing, and a host of other differences" (p. 130). As a classroom teacher, there were instances when I assumed parental consent or understanding implicitly, without asking if this was the case. Collaborative dialogue is the only way to accurately member check another's beliefs, and I hold this incredibly close in my current practice as an educator, researcher, and leader. Using this grounding assumption as a starting point, I first focused on the narratives of the families, with the intention of conducting participatory research that involved a cycle of inquiry. By employing a participatory design, I hoped to contribute viable approaches that address the critical issues arising in the field of special education (Merriam, 2009). Each of the cycles of research involved parents of students who receive special education services, in addition to special education staff. In this section, I outline the setting, collaborators in the inquiry, and methods that support this research.

RESEARCH QUESTIONS

- What are the experiences of culturally and linguistically diverse (CLD) families navigating special education in a public school district?

- How can an understanding of CLD families' experiences inform the practices of special education teams?
- How do families describe

   - their child? What does their child like? What are their strengths?
   - their initial contact with special education staff?
   - their understanding of the special education assessment process?
   - their ongoing communication with special education staff?
   - their understanding of the special education paperwork?
   - the role they play in the designing and monitoring of their child's educational program?

- Based on parent narratives, how might we consider

   - the ways in which we initially contact families?
   - the ways in which we share the assessment process?
   - the ways in which we model and support ongoing communication?
   - the ways in which we facilitate understanding of the special education paperwork?
   - the roles that parents play in the designing and monitoring of their child's educational program?

- How can district staff work to effect change to the procedures of the special education department of a public school district to address the needs of culturally and linguistically diverse (CLD) families?
- How do special education teams contribute to the cultivation of social capital among the families they serve?
- How do we develop teams that recognize and support the further development of the community cultural wealth of students and families that receive special education services?

RESEARCH DESIGN

The purpose of this research was to gain an understanding of the experiences of CLD families of students with IEPs in the effort to center their voices and move collaboratively toward eliminating the barriers that exist between effective and meaningful communication in the IEP process. Through the cycle of inquiry, this research also aimed to engage special education staff in a critical reflection on the experiences of CLD families, to (re)consider practices that involve parents and families of students with IEPs while using the methodologies of participatory action research (PAR). PAR is the process in which the scholar-practitioner engages in a cycle of inquiry and action with the community in order to address a specific situation or problem that arises from an imbalance of power or inequitable dispersal of material resources, power, and privilege (Anderson et al., 2007). As described by De Schutter and Yopo (1981), the community and the researcher collaboratively produce critical understanding of the problem in order to produce transformational change. Schwandt (1997) describes the origins of action research, dating back to Kurt Lewin in the 1940s. Participatory research in Latin America during the 1960s and 1970s was more inclusive of the peoples and communities that were impacted by the problems of practice, as well as the intended research and outcomes. Freire (1970), in collaborating with the participants in research related to adult literacy, expanded the definition of a researcher to include those who directly benefit from the work. Participatory action research integrated theory and practice. The basic tenets of action research, including PAR, are the interconnected cycles of questioning, collaborating, reflecting, and acting. Similarly, Esposito and Evans-Winters (2022) describe intersectional research methodology as "contemplating, interrogating, naming, and simultaneously reclaiming and rejecting that nexus between the *known and unknown, invisible and (hyper)visible,* and *humanizing and dehumanizing*" (p. 4). It is the obligation of every researcher to be intentional and intersectional in their work, and I strive to accomplish the aims put forth by these two exemplary scholars.

Hendricks's (2017) discussion of collaborative action research includes the idea that legitimate knowledge is expanded to include those members of the research team who have traditionally had research done *for* and *on* them, yet rarely have the opportunity to participate in the process *by which* they are themselves the researcher. This is particularly of importance in the field of special education. Bruce and Pine (2010) argue that action research is well suited to tackle the systemic issues in special education as its "recursive quality creates opportunities for teachers to change their instructional focus or approach in response to new understandings that emerge from multiple cycles of reflection and action" (p. 16).

Utilizing a grounded theory approach (Strauss & Corbin, 1994), this participatory research is deconstructed into four points in the cycle: *questioning, collaborating, reflecting,* and *acting*. The roadmap for this study follows:

- *Questioning*: My research questions evolved over my three years as a doctoral student at California State University, East Bay. During the spring semester of 2020, I had the opportunity to participate in a pilot study with one of my special education teacher interns. Many of our conversations focused on issues regarding parent participation and equity. While she continued her work in a master's in special education program at a local university, she ultimately made the decision to return to a general education position for the 2020–21 school year. I viewed our work together as coconspirators, and have yet to find a colleague in my department that I connect with as deeply in the area of education for social justice. This required a rethinking of my research, which brings the experiences of CLD families to the center of the conversation. Utilizing feedback and advice from members of my critical friends (Anderson et al., 2007), reflection on the previous work, as well as suggestions from my dissertation chair, the research questions expanded in both depth and clarity to truly align to my personal values and reasons for doing this work.
- *Collaborating*: During this cycle, I engaged in dialogue with eleven parents of students with IEPs in a public school district, as well as the matriculating high school district. I required language interpretation in order to dialogue with three of the collaborators; however, six of the eleven families speak an additional language in the home. One household was trilingual. In addition to the eleven parent dialogues, I conducted two focus groups with district special education staff, one with five participants, and the other with four. I selected four quotes from the parent dialogues with the intention of eliciting conversation centered on enacting change to current policies and procedures.
- *Reflecting*: I view reflection as running parallel to the other three steps in action. I aim to have a shared ownership with my collaborators. I intentionally reflected on my work and experiences using the frameworks of community cultural wealth and disability studies in education. Anderson et al. (2007) state that "action research is done within an action-oriented setting in which reflection on action is the driving force of the research" (p. xix). I utilized reflexive journaling after my dialogues, and following the focus groups with the special education staff. The reflexive journal was key to ensuring that the research remained on track, keeping the spirit of the research questions and my rationale for initiating the process alive.

- *Acting*: The narratives that emerged from this study serve as a product on their own. In addition to this, the parent narratives assist with the reconceptualization of special education to serve culturally and linguistically diverse families in a more equitable and just process. I veered away from the notion of producing something specific for special education staff at the onset of this research, in that this would be in contradiction of the tenets of participatory research, as well as grounded theory. Much as special education law dictates that school districts not predetermine services for students with disabilities, it was my place to predetermine a tangible outcome.

It is through this process that I intentionally work in the name of social justice and equity.

SETTING

The school district serves approximately 10,500 students from preschool through eighth grade in two cities located in Northern California. There are twenty-two school campuses within the district: one preschool complex, fifteen elementary (TK–5) schools, three TK (transitional kindergarten) through eighth grade schools, and three middle (6–8 grade) schools. Tables A.1 and A.2 provide us with useful student demographics.

Within the school district, the special education department serves approximately 9 percent of the district's enrollment with IEPs. The

TABLE A.1. Race/Ethnicity Breakdown

Race/Ethnicity	Percentage
African American/Black	0.7 percent
American Indian	0.1 percent
Asian	25.9 percent
Filipino	3.4 percent
Hispanic/Latino	36.6 percent
Two or More Races	9.4 percent
Pacific Islander	2.1 percent
White	21 percent
Not reported	0.8 percent

Source: California School Dashboard (https://www.caschooldashboard.org/).

TABLE A.2. Student Demographics

Student Demographics	Percentage
English Learners	22.9 percent
Foster Youth	0.1 percent
Homeless	2.3 percent
Socioeconomically Disadvantaged	30.8 percent
Students with Disabilities	8.8 percent

Source: California School Dashboard (https://www.caschooldashboard.org/).

department offers a full range of services: specialized academic instruction (SAI) by a credentialed education specialist; speech, occupational (OT), and physical therapy (PT); behavior support and interventions, applied behavioral analysis (ABA), adaptive physical education (APE), assistive technology (AT), alternative and augmentative communication, (AAC), vision services, orientation and mobility (O&M), special circumstance instructional assistance (SCIA), and nursing. The school district employs approximately sixty credentialed special education teachers, eighteen school psychologists, and approximately forty related service providers. There are six department administrators: a director of special education, an assistant director of special education, and four coordinators who oversee programs across the district. Additionally, there is a district office-based program specialist who provides additional assistance to schools and teams.

The IEP process in the district follows the legal mandates outlined by IDEA, as well as the California Education Code. Students are referred for special education assessment either by parents, an outside agency, or through the school-based student study team (SST). Once a student is determined to be eligible for special education services under an IEP, meetings are held at least annually to report on present levels of performance, progress on goals, and a district offer of services. In addition to this, a reevaluation to determine continued eligibility for special education is held every three years. Parents and guardians have the right to call an IEP meeting throughout the school year, and the team must meet within thirty calendar days of the request. IEPs are also held in anticipation of transitions from one school to another (preschool to elementary, elementary to middle, middle to high), as well as to address issues surrounding behavior and suspensions through a manifest determination

(MD) meeting. The IEP team is generally composed of the parents, a general education teacher, a special education teacher, related service providers, and an administrative designee who can commit district resources in the meeting. Some meetings require the presence of a school psychologist, and in upper elementary and middle school the student is asked to participate as well.

COLLABORATORS

In describing the foundational work in action research by John Collier and Kurt Lewin, Bruce and Pine (2010) state that "they viewed action research as a collaborative process in which participants could work together to understand and solve social and organizational problems by conducting studies of their own situations and circumstances" (p. 6).

In keeping with the spirit of action research, in lieu of using the traditional term *participants*, I refer to those undertaking the research with me as my *collaborators*. During my time as a program specialist in the school district, I had the opportunity to work with some inspirational staff and families. During the spring of 2020, as I was engaging in my pilot study, I sought out one educator and one parent to work with. Brief descriptions of these individuals follow.

Mia

Mia is a Jordanian and Syrian American woman who worked in two elementary schools as a case manager and resource specialist. While the 2019–20 school year was her first year in the resource specialist program (RSP) position, she had previously taught in the district as a general education first- and second-grade teacher for four years. During the time of the research, she was enrolled in a dual preliminary education specialist credentialing and master's degree program at a local public university. During the 2019–20 school year, I served as her intern mentor, and many of our conversations were centered on the barriers that educators and parents face in building partnership during the special education process. Mia was excited to undertake this research with me, both as a collaborator and a critical friend (Anderson et al., 2007); however, at the end of the 2019–20 school year she decided to return to the general education classroom, citing personal anxiety over not being able to adequately serve her students and families.

Aida

Aida is an Iranian American woman with a son enrolled in a local private school that specializes in serving students on the autism spectrum. Previously, her son was enrolled in district schools, first in the RSP program and then in a self-contained special day class (SDC). I worked with Aida throughout my initial five years with the district, as her son changed schools and settings. Aida works for a nonprofit organization geared toward lobbying major publishing houses to print children's books that celebrate diverse cultures and traditions.

INSTRUMENTS AND DATA COLLECTION

Data was collected through dialogues and focus groups. The data worked in conjunction to support the understanding of how CLD families describe their experiences and how district special education leadership considers parent narratives to enact change to more equitably serve culturally and linguistically diverse families in special education.

Data Collection Method #1: Dialogues

During the *collaborating* portion of the inquiry cycle, I engaged CLD parents of students with IEPs in dialogues. I intentionally utilize the term *dialogue* instead of *interview* in order to both name and disrupt the power dynamic that is associated with the concept of interviews. Conversations are an effective way to gain understanding about the lives and experiences of collaborators (Rubin & Rubin, 2011), which is a goal of participatory research and the iterative cycle of inquiry. As Anderson et al. (2007) states, this involves "tapping multiple perspectives to get a firm sense of the issues being tackled and to craft a plan that reflects these multiple perspectives" (p. 146). The goal of the parent dialogues was to gather data to answer the research questions related to the lived experiences of CLD families. Participants for dialogue were selected through purposeful sampling (Merriam, 2009), based on my prior relationships and their involvement in the special education process, as well as reflecting a diverse range of experiences within the district community. Bringing parents into the cycle of research as collaborators involves creating a transparent and open line of communication. The dialogue sessions were semistructured in nature, which gave the participants in the dialogue the ability to probe or ask follow-up and clarifying questions (Merriam, 2009). Dialogue sessions were conducted via Zoom video conferencing due to the ongoing COVID-19 pandemic. All sessions were recorded and transcribed. Dialogue protocols for parent dialogue sessions can be found in appendix C. These questions focus on the speaker's experience with the special education process, from describing their child and speaking to the student's strengths and areas of interest, through initial contact with special education staff and the assessment process, ongoing communication with staff, their understanding of special education paperwork, and their understanding of the role they play in determining their child's IEP and education.

Data Collection Method #2: Focus Groups

In conversations with colleagues, as well as in my own reflections, I determined that it was essential to hear directly from special education leaders to consider how our work with CLD families can shift after hearing excerpts of parent narratives that will emerge from the dialogues. The focus groups contributed to the answering of the second research question: How can an understanding of CLD families' experiences inform the practices of special education teams? The establishment of conditions conducive to this work is the beginning of an emancipatory activity that aims to support conversations around issues of equity and change.

STRENGTHS AND LIMITATIONS/ TRUSTWORTHINESS

It is my belief that the strengths and limitations of participatory research are actually one and the same. Action research, unlike traditional research, is not generalizable in the way that many academics are used to and feel comfortable with (Anderson et al., 2007); however, it is transferable (Lincoln & Guba, 1985). Transferability implies that research and its findings can be applied to different situations after careful consideration of contextual factors. For example, while this research is conducted in the suburban San Francisco Bay Area, a teacher practitioner in a different setting could utilize some of the instruments and methods, but would need to identify how their setting differs. The same results would not be expected, as the participants and the unique data sets are limited to the educators and families of my school district.

In order to establish the trustworthiness of the research, multiple sources of data were collected, as described in the section above. In addition to this, the perspectives of multiple stakeholders were collected in order to furnish diverse viewpoints and responses to the research questions. Therefore, with this triangulation of the data, the research can be assumed to be valid for the environment and situation in which it was gathered (Shenton, 2004). Furthermore, all of the participants in this study were recruited voluntarily and were informed that they may end their participation at any time. All participants were provided with notice that their names and identities will be kept confidential, minimizing the potential risks to the participants.

Appendix B
Acronym Glossary

AAC: alternative and augmentative communication
AB: assembly bill
ABA: applied behavior analysis
ADHD: attention deficit hyperactivity disorder
ADR: Alternative Dispute Resolution
AP: asset pedagogy
APE: adaptive physical education
ASD: autism spectrum disorder
ASL: American Sign Language
AT: assistive technology
AUT: autism
BCBA: board certified behavior analyst
BEA: Bilingual Education Act
BIP: behavior intervention plan
BT: behavioral technician
BT: behavioral therapist
CBO: community-based organization
CCS: California Children's Services
CCW: community cultural wealth
CDE: California Department of Education
CLD: culturally and linguistically diverse
COE: county office of education
CRP: culturally responsive pedagogy
CRT: critical race theory
CSP: culturally sustaining pedagogy
DELAC: district English learner advisory committee
DI: differentiated instruction
DIY: do-it-yourself

DNQ: do not qualify
DSE: disability studies in education
DSM: Diagnostic and Statistical Manual of Mental Disorders
EAHCA: Education for All Handicapped Children Act
ED: emotional disturbance
EHA: Education of the Handicapped Act
EI: early intervention
ELAC: English Learner Advisory Committee
ELL: English language learner
EO: English only
ERMHS: Educationally Related Mental Health Services
ESEA: Elementary and Secondary Education Act
ESSA: Every Student Succeeds Act
FAPE: free, appropriate, public education
FBA: functional behavioral assessment
FERPA: Family Educational Rights and Privacy Act
FIEP: Facilitated Individualized Education Plan
GGRC: Golden Gate Regional Center
ID: intellectual disability
IDEA: Individuals with Disabilities Education Act
IEP: Individualized Education Plan
IFSP: Individualized Family Service Plan
IHO: impartial hearing officer
LCAP: local control accountability plan
LD: learning disability
LEA: local educational agency
LEP: limited English proficient
LRE: least restrictive environment
MD: manifest determination
MD: multiple disability
NPS: nonpublic school
OCR: Office of Civil Rights
ODD: oppositional defiant disorder
OHI: other health impairment
O&M: orientation and mobility
OT: occupational therapy
PAR: participatory action research
PD: professional development
PDF: portable document format

PLC: professional learning community
PT: physical therapy
PTA: parent-teacher association
PTO: Parent-Teacher Organization
ROI: release of information
RSP: resource specialist program
SAI: specialized academic instruction
SCIA: special circumstance instructional assistance
SDC: special day class
SEA: state education agency
SEDAC: Special Education District Advisory Council
SEIS: Special Education Information System
SELPAs: Special Education Local Planning Areas
SDC: special day class
SIP: school improvement plan
SIRAS: SELPA Information Records and Analysis Support
SLD: specific learning disability
SLI: speech and language impairment
SLP: speech-language pathologist
SSC: school site council
SST: student study team/student success team
TDC: therapeutic day class
TSDC: therapeutic special day class
TK: transitional kindergarten
UDL: universal design for learning

Appendix C
Parent Dialogue Protocol

- Please tell me about your child.
    - What does your child like?
    - What are your child's strengths?

- Please tell me about your first discussion with a teacher about your child's learning differences.
- Please tell me about your first contact with special education.
- Please tell me about how your child was first assessed for special education services.
- Please tell me about your ongoing communication with special education staff.
- Please tell me about how you receive special education paperwork from your child's school.
- Please tell me how the special education paperwork is explained by your child's teachers and other staff.
- Please tell me about your expectations for your child's special education services.
- Please tell me about the role you play in the designing and monitoring of your child's educational program.

FOCUS GROUP PROTOCOL

Based on parent narratives, how might we (special education teams) consider

- the ways we can learn from parents about their child's assets, strengths, and interests?

- the ways in which we engage families about a child's learning differences?
- the ways in which we initially contact families?
- the ways in which we share the assessment process?
- the ways in which we model and support ongoing communication?
- the ways in which we facilitate understanding of the special education paperwork?
- the expectations that parents have about their child's special education services?
- the roles that parents play in the designing and monitoring of their child's educational program?

References

Anderson, G. L., Herr, K., & Nihlen, A. S. (Eds.). (2007). *Studying your own school: An educator's guide to practitioner action research*. Corwin Press.

Annamma, S. A. (2017). *The pedagogy of pathologization: Dis/abled girls of color in the school-prison nexus*. Routledge.

Annamma, S. A., Connor, D., & Ferri, B. (2013). Dis/ability critical race studies (DisCrit): Theorizing at the intersections of race and dis/ability. *Race Ethnicity and Education, 16*(1), 1–31.

Annamma, S. A., Ferri, B. A., & Connor, D. J. (Eds.). (2022). *DisCrit expanded: Reverberations, ruptures, and inquiries*. Teachers College Press.

Bacon, J. K., & Causton-Theoharis, J. (2013). "'It should be teamwork': A critical investigation of school practices and parent advocacy in special education." *International Journal of Inclusive Education, 17*(7), 682–699.

Bakken, J. P., & Smith, B. A. (2011). A blueprint for developing culturally proficient/responsive school administrators in special education. *Learning Disabilities: A Contemporary Journal, 9*(1), 33–46.

Baglieri, S., Bejoian, L. M., Broderick, A. A., Connor, D. J., & Valle, J. (2011). Inviting interdisciplinary alliances around inclusive educational reform: Introduction to the special issue on disability studies in education. *Teachers College Record, 113*(10), 2115–2121.

Baglieri, S., & Knopf, J. H. (2004). Normalizing difference in inclusive teaching. *Journal of Learning Disabilities, 37*(6), 525–529.

Baglieri, S., Valle, J. W., Connor, D. J., & Gallagher, D. J. (2011). Disability studies in education: The need for a plurality of perspectives on disability. *Remedial and Special Education, 32*(4), 267–278.

Bateman, B. D. (2017). Individual education programs for children with disabilities. In J. M. Kauffman, D. P. Hallahan, & P. Cullen Pullen (Eds.), *Handbook of special education* (2nd ed., pp. 87–104). Routledge.

Bejarano, C., & Valverde, M. (2013). From the fields to the university: Charting educational access and success for farmworker students using a Community Cultural Wealth framework. *Association of Mexican American Educators Journal, 6*(2), 22–29.

Bill Text AB-2657 Pupil discipline: Restraint and seclusion. (2017–2018). Bill Text—AB-2657 Pupil discipline: restraint and seclusion. (2018, October 1). Retrieved November 12, 2022, from https://leginfo.legislature.ca.gov/faces/billNavClient.xhtml?bill_id=201720180AB2657.

Bourdieu, P. (2011/1986). *The forms of capital*. Routledge.

Bruce, S., & Pine, G. (2010). *Action research in special education*. Teachers College Press.

Burciaga, R., & Erbstein, N. (2013). Latina/o dropouts: Generating community cultural wealth. *Association of Mexican American Educators Journal, 6*(1), 24–33.

Burke, M., & Goldman, S. (2015). Identifying the associated factors of mediation and due process in families of students with autism spectrum disorder. *Journal of Autism & Developmental Disorders, 45*(5), 1345–1353.

CalEdFacts. (2023). *Fingertip facts on education in California*. Retrieved February 6, 2023, from https://www.cde.ca.gov/ds/sd/cb/ceffingertipfacts.asp.

California School Dashboard. (2023). Retrieved February 6, 2023, from https://www.caschooldashboard.org/reports/ca/2022.

Capper, C. A. (2018). *Organizational theory for equity and diversity: Leading integrated, socially just education*. Routledge.

Chang, A., Torrez, M. A., Ferguson, K. N., & Sagar, A. (2017). Figured worlds and American dreams: An exploration of agency and identity among Latinx undocumented students. *The Urban Review, 49*(2), 189–216.

CodeStack. (2020). SEIS Special Education Information Systems. https://www.seis.org/images/MapUpdate_November2020.pdf.

Collier, M., Keefe, E. B., & Hirrel, L. A. (2015). Listening to parents' narratives: The value of authentic experiences with children with disabilities and the families. *School Community Journal, 25*(2), 221–242.

Connor, D. J., Gabel, S. L., Gallagher, D. J., & Morton, M. (2008). Disability studies and inclusive education—Implications for theory, research, and practice. *International Journal of Inclusive Education, 12*(5–6), 441–457.

Connor, D. J., Ferri, B., & Annamma, S. A. (Eds.) (2016). *DisCrit: Disability studies and critical race theory in education*. Teachers College Press.

Crenshaw, K. (1990). Mapping the margins: Intersectionality, identity politics, and violence against women of color. *Stanford Law Review, 43*(6), 1241–1299.

Danforth, S. (2006). Learning from our historical evasions: Disability studies and schooling in a liberal democracy. In S. Danforth & S. L. Gabel (Eds.), *Vital questions facing disability studies in education* (pp. 77–90). Peter Lange Inc.

DeNicolo, C. P., González, M., Morales, S., & Romaní, L. (2015). Teaching through testimonio: Accessing community cultural wealth in school. *Journal of Latinos and Education, 14*(4), 228–243.

De Schutter, A., & Yopo, B. (1981). *Investigacion participativa: Una opcion metodologica para la education de adultos*. Pátzcuaro, Michoacán, México: CREFAL.

Dweck, C. S. (2008). *Mindset: The new psychology of success*. Ballantine Books.

Dwyer, S. C., & Buckle, J. L. (2009). The space between: On being an insider-outsider in qualitative research. *International journal of qualitative methods, 8*(1), 54–63.

Duffy-Sherr, K. (2021). *What do families and case managers really think about the IEP process? A mixed methods approach* [Unpublished doctoral dissertation. California State University, East Bay].

EdData District Profile. (2023, February). Retrieved February 23, 2023, from http://www.ed-data.org/district/San-Mateo/San-Mateo--Foster-City.

Edwards, C. C., & Da Fonte, A. (2012). The 5-point plan: Fostering successful partnerships with families of students with disabilities. *Teaching Exceptional Children, 44*(3), 6–13.

Esposito, J., & Evans-Winters, V. (2022). *Introduction to intersectional qualitative research*. SAGE Publications.

Evans-Santiago, B. (Ed.). (2020). *Mistakes we have made: Implications for social justice educators*. Myers Education Press.

Fenton, P., Ocasio-Stoutenburg, L., & Harry, B. (2017). The power of parent engagement: Sociocultural considerations in the quest for equity. *Theory into Practice, 56*(3), 214–225.

Ferguson, P. M., & Nusbaum, E. (2012). Disability studies: What is it and what difference does it make? *Research and Practice for Persons with Severe Disabilities, 37*(2), 70–80.

Fernández, E., & Paredes Scribner, S. M. (2018). "Venimos para que se oiga la voz": Activating community cultural wealth as parental educational leadership. *Journal of Research on Leadership Education, 13*(1), 59–78.

Ferri, B. A., & Connor, D. J. (2006). *Reading resistance: Discourses of exclusion in desegregation & inclusion debates* (vol. 1). Peter Lang.

Fitzgerald, J. L., & Watkins, M. W. (2006). Parents' rights in special education: The readability of procedural safeguards. *Exceptional Children, 72*(4), 497–510.

Foronda, C., Baptiste, D. L., Reinholdt, M. M., & Ousman, K. (2016). Cultural humility: A concept analysis. *Journal of Transcultural Nursing, 27*(3), 210–217.

Freedman, M. K. (2017). *Special education 2.0: Breaking taboos to build a new education law*. School Law Pro.

Freire, P. (1970). *Pedagogy of the oppressed*. Continuum.

Fullan, M. (2007). *Leading in a culture of change*. John Wiley & Sons.

Gallo, S. (2017). *Mi padre: Mexican immigrant fathers and their children's education*. Teachers College Press.

Gándara, P., Losen, D., August, D., Uriarte, M., Gómez, M. C., & Hopkins, M. (2010). Forbidden language: A brief history of US language policy. In P. Gándara & M. Hopkins (Eds.), *Forbidden language: English learners and restrictive language policies* (pp. 20–33). Teachers College Press.

Gándara, P., Maxwell-Jolly, J., Garcia, E., Asato, J., Gutierrez, K., Stritikus, T., & Curry, J. (2000). (rep). *The initial impact of Proposition 227 on the instruction of English learners*. Linguistic Minority Research Institute, Education Policy Center, University of California, Davis.

Gándara, P., Moran, R., & Garcia, E. (2004). Chapter 2: Legacy of Brown: Lau and language policy in the United States. *Review of Research in Education, 28*(1), 27–46.

Gardner, J. E., Scherman, A., Mobley, D., Brown, P., & Schutter, M. (1994). Grandparents' beliefs regarding their role and relationship with special needs grandchildren. *Education and Treatment of Children, 17*(2), 185–196.

Gonzales, S. M., & Gabel, S. L. (2017). Exploring involvement expectations for culturally and linguistically diverse parents: What we need to know in teacher education. *International Journal of Multicultural Education, 19*(2), 61–81.

Gray, S. A., Zraick, R. I., & Atcherson, S. R. (2019). Readability of individuals with disabilities education act part B procedural safeguards: An update. *Language, speech, and hearing services in schools, 50*(3), 373–384.

Gregg, K., Rugg, M., & Stoneman, Z. (2012). Building on the hopes and dreams of Latino families with young children: Findings from family member focus groups. *Early Childhood Education Journal, 40*(2), 87–96.

Griffith, M. (2015). A look at funding for students with disabilities. *The Progress of Education Reform, 16*(1), 1–6.

Hagiwara, M., & Shogren, K. A. (2018). Collaborate with families to support student learning and secure needed services. In J. McLeskey, L. Maheady, B. Billingsley, M. Brownell, & Tim Lewis (Eds.), *High leverage practices for inclusive classrooms* (pp. 34–47). Routledge.

Hammond, Z. (2014). *Culturally responsive teaching and the brain: Promoting authentic engagement and rigor among culturally and linguistically diverse students*. Corwin Press.

Hanson, M. J., & Lynch, E. W. (2004). *Understanding families: Approaches to diversity, disability, and risk*. Paul H Brookes Publishing Co.

Harris, B., McClain, M. B., Haverkamp, C. R., Cruz, R. A., Benallie, K. J., & Benney, C. M. (2019). School-based assessment of autism spectrum disorder among culturally and linguistically diverse children. *Professional Psychology: Research and Practice, 50*(5), 323.

Harry, B. (2008). Collaboration with culturally and linguistically diverse families: Ideal versus reality. *Exceptional Children, 74*(3), 372–388.

Harry, B., & Klingner, J. (2014). *Why are so many minority students in special education?* Teachers College Press.

Harry, B., & Ocasio-Stoutenburg, L. (2020). *Meeting families where they are: Building equity through advocacy with diverse schools and communities*. Disability, Culture, and Equity.

Hendricks, C. C. (2017). *Improving schools through action research: A reflective practice approach*. Pearson.

Herrera, S. G., Porter, L., & Barko-Alva, K. (2020). *Equity in school–parent partnerships: Cultivating community and family trust in culturally diverse classrooms*. Teachers College Press.

Hess, R. S., Molina, A. M., & Kozleski, E. B. (2006). Until somebody hears me: Parent voice and advocacy in special educational decision-making. *British Journal of Special Education, 33*(3), 148–157.

Hook, J. N., Davis, D. E., Owen, J., Worthington Jr., E. L., & Utsey, S. O. (2013). Cultural humility: Measuring openness to culturally diverse clients. *Journal of Counseling Psychology, 60*(3), 353.

hooks, b. (1994). *Teaching to transgress*. Routledge.

Hughes, M. T., Valle-Riestra, D. M., & Arguelles, M. E. (2002). Experiences of Latino families with their child's special education program. *Multicultural Perspectives, 4*(1), 11–17.

Hyman, E., Rivkin, D. H., & Rosenbaum, S. A. (2011). How IDEA fails families without means: Causes and corrections from the frontlines of special education lawyering. *Journal of Gender, Social Policy, & The Law, 20*(1), 107–162.

Ishimaru, A. M. (2020). *Just schools: Building equitable collaborations with families and communities*. Teachers College Press.

Jung, A. W. (2011). Individualized education programs (IEPs) and barriers for parents from culturally and linguistically diverse backgrounds. *Multicultural Education, 18*(3), 21–25.

Kalyanpur, M., & Harry, B. (2012). *Cultural reciprocity in special education: Building family–professional relationships*. Paul H. Brooks.

Kania, J., Kramer, M., & Senge, P. (2018). (rep.). *The water of systems change*. FSG. https://www.fsg.org/publications/water_of_systems_change.

Katsiyannis, A., Yell, M. L., & Bradley, R. (2001). Reflections on the 25th anniversary of the Individuals with Disabilities Education Act. *Remedial and Special Education*, 22(6), 324–334.

Katz, S., & Kessel, L. (2002). Grandparents of children with developmental disabilities: Perceptions, beliefs, and involvement in their care. *Issues in Comprehensive Pediatric Nursing*, 25(2), 113–128.

Kutner, M., Greenberg, E., & Baer, J. (2006). A first look at the literacy of America's adults in the 21st century (Report No. NCES 2006-470). National Center for Education Statistics.

Ladson-Billings, G. (1992). Culturally relevant teaching: The key to making multicultural education work. In C. A. Grant (Ed.), *Research and multicultural education: From the margins to the mainstream* (pp. 106–121). Falmer Press.

Ladson-Billings, G. (1995a). But that's just good teaching! The case for culturally relevant pedagogy. *Theory into practice*, 34(3), 159–165.

Ladson-Billings, G. (1995b). Toward a theory of culturally relevant pedagogy. *American Educational Research Journal*, 32(3), 465–491.

Ladson-Billings, G. (2006). From the achievement gap to the education debt: Understanding achievement in US schools. *Educational researcher*, 35(7), 3–12.

Ladson-Billings, G. (2014). Culturally relevant pedagogy 2.0: Aka the remix. *Harvard Educational Review*, 84(1), 74–84.

Ladson-Billings, G. (2021). *Culturally relevant pedagogy: Asking a different question*. Teachers College Press.

Lai, Y., & Vadeboncoeur, J. A. (2013). The discourse of parent involvement in special education: A critical analysis linking policy documents to the experiences of mothers. *Educational Policy*, 27(6), 867–897.

Lalvani, P. (2012). Parents' participation in special education in the context of implicit educational ideologies and socioeconomic status. *Education and Training in Autism and Developmental Disabilities*, 474–486.

Lalvani, P. (2013). Privilege, compromise, or social justice: Teachers' conceptualizations of inclusive education. *Disability & Society*, 28(1), 14–27.

Larios, R., & Zetlin, A. (2022). Bilingual and monolingual parents' counterstories of the individualized education program (IEP) meeting. *Urban Education*, 57(7), 1207–1229.

Larios, R., & Zetlin, A. (2012). Parental involvement and participation of monolingual and bilingual Latino Families during the Individual Education program meetings. *Journal of Education Research*, 6(3), 279–298.

Larrotta, C., & Yamamura, E. K. (2011). A community cultural wealth approach to Latina/Latino parent involvement: The promise of family literacy. *Adult Basic Education and Literacy Journal*, 5(2), 74–83.

Lasky, B., & Karge, B. D. (2011). Involvement of language minority parents of children with disabilities in their child's school achievement. *Multicultural Education*, 19(3), 29–34.

Lincoln, Y. S., & Guba, E. G. (1985). *Naturalistic inquiry*. SAGE.

Lo, L. (2008). Chinese families' level of participation and experiences in IEP meetings. *Preventing School Failure: Alternative Education for Children and Youth*, 53(1), 21–27.

Lo, L. (2012). Demystifying the IEP process for diverse parents of children with disabilities. *Teaching Exceptional Children, 44*(3), 14–20.

Love, B. L. (2019). *We want to do more than survive: Abolitionist teaching and the pursuit of educational freedom.* Beacon Press.

Mandic, C. G., Rudd, R., Hehir, T., & Acevedo-Garcia, D. (2012). Readability of special education procedural safeguards. *The Journal of Special Education, 45*(4), 195–203.

Mapp, K. L., & Kuttner, P. J. (2013). *Partners in education: A dual capacity-building framework for family-school partnerships.* Sedl.

Martin, P. (1995). Proposition 187 in California. *International Migration Review, 29*(1), 255–263.

Martínez-Álvarez, P. (2020). Dis/ability as mediator: Opportunity encounters in hybrid learning spaces for emergent bilinguals with dis/abilities. *Teachers College Record, 122*(5), 1–44.

McCarthy Foubert, J. L. (2022). *Reckoning with racism in family-school partnerships: Centering Black parents' school engagement.* Teachers College Press.

McCloskey, E. (2022). *A world away from IEPs: How disabled students learn in out-of-school spaces.* Teachers College Press.

McGinley, V. A., & Alexander, M. (Eds.). (2017). *Parents and families of students with special needs: Collaborating across the age span.* SAGE Publications.

McLeod, T. (2022). Parent-educator partnerships in special education services provision: A thematic exploration of challenges faced by culturally and linguistically diverse families. *International Journal of Special Education (IJSE), 37*(1).

McNaughton, D., & Vostal, B. R. (2010). Using active listening to improve collaboration with parents: The LAFF don't CRY strategy. *Intervention in School and Clinic, 45*(4), 251–256.

Merriam, S. B. (2009). *Qualitative research: A guide to design and implementation.* John Wiley & Sons.

Merton, R. K. (1972). Insiders and outsiders: A chapter in the sociology of knowledge. *American Journal of Sociology, 78*(1), 9–47.

More, C. M., Hart, J. E., & Cheatham, G. A. (2013). Language interpretation for diverse families: Considerations for special education teachers. *Intervention in School and Clinic, 49*(2), 113–120.

Mueller, T. G., & Buckley, P. C. (2014a). Fathers' experiences with the special education system: The overlooked voice. *Research and Practice for Persons with Severe Disabilities, 39*(2), 119–135.

Mueller, T. G., & Buckley, P. C. (2014b). The odd man out: How fathers navigate the special education system. *Remedial and Special Education, 35*(1), 40–49.

Mueller, T. G. & Carranza, F. (2011). An examination of special education due process hearings. *Journal of Disability Policy Studies, 22*(3), 131–139.

Mueller, T. G., Milian, M., & Lopez, M. I. (2009). Latina mothers' views of a parent-to-parent support group in the special education system. *Research and Practice for Persons with Severe Disabilities, 34*(3–4), 113–122.

Murray, L. (2017). *Humanizing family engagement with Latinx immigrant families.* [Unpublished manuscript]. University of San Francisco.

National Center for Education Statistics. (2022). Search for Public School Districts. Accessed December 29, 2022, from https://nces.ed.gov/ccd/districtsearch/index.asp.

Nava, P. E., & Lara, A. (2016). Reconceptualizing leadership in migrant communities: Latina/o parent leadership retreats as sites of community cultural wealth. *Association of Mexican American Educators Journal, 10*(3), 90–107.

Nicolarakis, O. D., English, A., & Lawyer, G. (2022). Black deaf gain: A guide to revisioning K–12 deaf education. In F. Waitoller & K. Thorius (Eds.), *Sustaining disabled youth* (pp. 59–73). Teachers College Press.

Nielsen, K. E. (2012). *A disability history of the United States*. Beacon Press.

Ocasio-Stoutenburg, L., & Harry, B. (2021). *Case studies in building equity through family advocacy in special education: A companion volume to meeting families where they are*. Teachers College Press.

Olivos, E. M. (2009). Collaboration with Latino families: A critical perspective of home-school interactions. *Intervention in School and Clinic, 45*(2), 109–115.

Olivos, E. M., Gallagher, R. J., & Aguilar, J. (2010). Fostering collaboration with culturally and linguistically diverse families of children with moderate to severe disabilities. *Journal of Educational and Psychological Consultation, 20*(1), 28–40.

Pacino, M. A., & Warren, S. R. (Eds.). (2022). *Building culturally responsive partnerships among schools, families, and communities*. Teachers College Press.

Paris, D. (2012). Culturally sustaining pedagogy: A needed change in stance, terminology, and practice. *Educational Researcher, 41*(3), 93–97.

Paris, D., & Alim, H. S. (Eds.). (2017). *Culturally sustaining pedagogies: Teaching and learning for justice in a changing world*. Teachers College Press.

Prince, A. M., & Gothberg, J. (2019). Seclusion and restraint of students with disabilities: A 1-year legal review. *Journal of Disability Policy Studies, 30*(2), 118–124.

Pushor, D. (2012). Tracing my research on parent engagement: Working to interrupt the story of school as protectorate. *Action in Teacher Education, 34*(5–6), 464–479.

Reynolds, R. (2010). "They think you're lazy," and Other Messages Black parents send their Black sons: An exploration of critical race theory in the examination of educational outcomes for Black males. *Journal of African American Males in Education, 1*(2), 144–163.

Rubin, H. J., & Rubin, I. S. (2011). *Qualitative interviewing: The art of hearing data*. SAGE Publications.

San Francisco Unified School District. (2023, January). Resources for Families. https://www.sfusd.edu/special-education-parent-rights-and-procedural-safeguards.

San Mateo County Office of Education. (2023, January). *Parent and community*. San Mateo County Office of Education. https://www.smcoe.org/about/san-mateo-county-selpa/parent-and-community.html.

San Mateo-Foster City Summary. (2022, December 7). Retrieved December 7, 2022, from https://www.caschooldashboard.org/reports/41690390000000/2021.

Santa Clara County Office of Education. (2023, January). *For parents & community*. https://www.sccoe.org/selpa/Pages/ParentsAndCommunity.aspx.

Sauer, J. S., & Rossetti, Z. (2019). *Affirming disability: Strengths-based portraits of culturally diverse families*. Teachers College Press.

Schilmoeller, G. L., & Baranowski, M. D. (1998). Intergenerational support in families with disabilities: Grandparents' perspectives. *Families in Society, 79*(5), 465–476.

Schwandt, T. A. (1997). *Qualitative inquiry: A dictionary of terms*. SAGE Publications.

Schweik, S. M. (2009). *The ugly laws*. New York University Press.

SELPA Administrators of California. (2023, February). *Community advisory committee and parent engagement*. https://selpa.info/info/parents-as-partners.

Shakespeare, T. (2006). The social model of disability. *The Disability Studies Reader*, 2, 197–204.

Shenton, A. K. (2004). Strategies for ensuring trustworthiness in qualitative research projects. *Education for Information*, 22(2), 63–75.

Slee, R., & Allan, J. (2001). Excluding the included: A reconsideration of inclusive education. *International Studies in Sociology of Education*, 11(2), 173–192.

Solórzano, D. G., & Yosso, T. J. (2002). Critical race methodology: Counter-storytelling as an analytical framework for education research. *Qualitative Inquiry*, 8(1), 23–44.

Spaulding, L. S., & Pratt, S. M. (2015). A review and analysis of the history of special education and disability advocacy in the United States. *American Educational History Journal*, 42(1/2), 91–109.

Strauss, A., & Corbin, J. (1994). Grounded theory methodology. *Handbook of Qualitative Research*, 17(1), 273–285.

Taylor, J., & Udang, L. (2016). Proposition 58: English proficiency. Multilingual education. "California education for a global economy initiative." *California Initiative Review*, 2016(1), 9.

Tervalon, M., & Murray-Garcia, J. (1998). Cultural humility versus cultural competence: A critical distinction in defining physician training outcomes in multicultural education. *Journal of Health Care for the Poor and Underserved*, 9(2), 117–125.

Thorius, K. A. K., & Tan, P. (2016). Expanding analysis of educational debt. *DisCrit: Disability Studies and Critical Race Theory in Education*, 87–97.

Trainor, A. A. (2010a). Diverse approaches to parent advocacy during special education home–school interactions: Identification and use of cultural and social capital. *Remedial and Special Education*, 31(1), 34–47.

Trainor, A. A. (2010b). Reexamining the promise of parent participation in special education: An analysis of cultural and social capital. *Anthropology & Education Quarterly*, 41(3), 245–263.

Trucios-Haynes, E. (2000). Why race matters: LatCrit theory and Latina/o racial identity. *Berkeley La Raza LJ*, 12(1), 1–42.

Tutwiler, S. W. (2017). *Teachers as collaborative partners: Working with diverse families and communities*. Routledge.

Vogel-Campbell, K. (2021). *"Are we really working together?": Engaging culturally and linguistically diverse families in special education*. California State University, East Bay.

Voulgarides, C. (2018). *Does compliance matter in special education?: IDEA and the hidden inequities of practice*. Teachers College Press.

Waitoller, F. R., & Thorius, K. K. (2016). Cross-pollinating culturally sustaining pedagogy and universal design for learning: Toward an inclusive pedagogy that accounts for dis/ability. *Harvard Educational Review*, 86(3), 366–389.

Waitoller, F. R., & Thorius, K. K. (Eds.). (2022). *Sustaining disabled youth: Centering disability in asset pedagogies*. Teachers College Press.

Weber, M. (2013). Children with disabilities, parents without disabilities, and lawyers: Issues of life experience, affinity, and agency. In A. S. Kanter & B. A. Ferri (Eds.), *Righting educational wrongs: disability studies in law and education* (pp. 207–217). Syracuse University Press.

Wolfe, K., & Duran, L. K. (2013). Culturally and linguistically diverse parents' perceptions of the IEP process: A review of current research. *Multiple Voices for Ethnically Diverse Exceptional Learners, 13*(2), 4–18.

Wong, A. (Ed.). (2020). *Disability visibility: First-person stories from the twenty-first century*. Vintage.

Woods, I. L., & Graves, S. L. (2021). The fortieth anniversary of Larry PV Riles: Cognitive assessment and Black children. *Contemporary School Psychology, 25*(2), 137–139.

Wright, K. B., Shields, S. M., Black, K., & Waxman, H. C. (2018). The effects of teacher home visits on student behavior, student academic achievement, and parent involvement. *School Community Journal, 28*(1), 67–90.

Yell, M. L., Bateman, D. F., & Shriner, J. G. (2021). *Developing educationally meaningful and legally sound IEPs*. Rowman & Littlefield.

Yosso, T. J. (2005). Whose culture has capital? A critical race theory discussion of community cultural wealth. *Race Ethnicity and Education, 8*(1), 69–91.

Zetlin, V. M., & Curcic, S. (2014). Parental voices on individualized education programs: "Oh, IEP meeting tomorrow? Rum tonight!" *Disability & Society, 29*(3), 373–387.

Index

AAC. *See* alternative and augmentative communication
AB329. *See* California Healthy Youth Act
AB 1266. *See* School Success and Opportunity Act
AB2657. *See* Assembly Bill 2657
ABA. *See* applied behavior analysis therapy
academics: expectations in, 51; language in, 4; SAI, 50, 72, 104–5, 164; soft classes, 121
accommodations, 3, 49, 132
acronyms, in IEPs, 151
acting, 163
adaptive physical education (APE), 65, 68, 164
ADHD. *See* attention deficit hyperactivity disorder
administrative credentialing program, 52
adoption, 67
ADR. *See* Alternative Dispute Resolution
advisory groups, 62
advocate, for family, 69, 81–82, 91–92
aggression, 51
Aida, 121–28, 166
alternative and augmentative communication (AAC), 85, 164
Alternative Dispute Resolution (ADR), 154
American Asylum for the Deaf, 6
American Education Research Association, 35
American Sign Language (ASL), 85

anthropology, 35; cultural, 11
antiracist framework, 12
anxiety, 12, 38, 96, 99, 109
APE. *See* adaptive physical education
applied behavior analysis (ABA) therapy, 52, 79, 123, 164
ASD. *See* autism spectrum disorder
ASL. *See* American Sign Language
aspirational capital, 29, 32, 140
Assembly Bill 2657 (AB2657), 91
assets-based: approach, 149; framework, 29; language, 39; learning, 137; thinking, 139, 149
assistive technology (AT), 50, 54, 164
asynchronous learning days, 59
AT. *See* assistive technology
attention deficit hyperactivity disorder (ADHD), 70, 96–97
autism (AUT), 50, 70, 74, 79, 100–101, 121
autism spectrum disorder (ASD), 11, 46, 51, 78
autonomy, 6

BCBA. *See* board-certified behavior analyst
BEA. *See* Bilingual Education Act
behavior, 110; ABA therapy, 52, 79, 123, 164; BCBA, 52; BIP, 76, 81–82, 98; BT, 12, 76, 82; development, 51; FBA, 81; intervention strategies, 137; support, 164
behavioral intervention plan (BIP), 76, 81–82, 98
behavioral technician (BT), 12
behavioral therapist (BT), 76, 82

Bell, Derrick, 30
Benson, Max, 91
bias, 16; implicit, 49, 147
biculturalism, 156
Bilingual Education Act (BEA), 9
bilingualism, 33, 100, 115, 156; in education, 9; in families, 16; in staff, 153
biliteracy, 33
BIP. *See* behavioral intervention plan
Black representation, 68
blindness, 85
board-certified behavior analyst (BCBA), 52
body regulation, 49
Bourdieu, Pierre, 30
BT. *See* behavioral technician; behavioral therapist
bullying, 105, 144
busing initiative, 68

California Anti-Discrimination Laws in Education Code, 108
California Children's Services (CCS), 84
California Department of Education (CDE), 19, 105
California Healthy Youth Act (AB 329), 108
California School Dashboard, 24
case managers, 20, 58, 69, 150–51
CBOs. *See* community-based organizations
CCS. *See* California Children's Services
CCW. *See* community cultural wealth
CDE. *See* California Department of Education
cerebral palsy, 84
cerumen impaction, 97
charter school, 95
civil rights movement, 35
classroom, 27, 144; community, 119; inclusive, 153; paraprofessional, 71, 82; physical environment of, 137; sizes, 107, 126; student running from, 51
CLD. *See* culturally and linguistically diverse families

Cler, Laurent, 6
COE. *See* County Office of Education
cognitive delays, 8
cognitive impairments, 84
collaboration, 32, 162
collaborative action research, 161
collaborative dialogue, 159
collaborator demographics, 43
collective problem-solving, 137, 139, 149
College Assistance Migrant Program, 34
Collier, John, 165
communication: AAC, 85, 164; collaboration and, 15, 20–21; lack of, 138; nonverbal, 136; resources for, 134; with school staff, 48, 116; styles, 128, 151; timelines, 92; verbal, 130
communicative competence, 16
communities: classroom, 119; of color, 29, 31; diverse, 49; migratory, 17; multigeneous, 27; PLCs, 22; resources, 62
community-based organizations (CBOs), 17, 156
community cultural wealth (CCW), 4, 29, 139; anatomy, 31; aspirational capital, 140; familial capital, 141; lineage, 30–31; linguistic capital, 140–41; navigational capital, 141–42; resistant capital, 142; social capital, 141
compliance, 15–19
convenience, of educator/school/district, 137, 146–74
core muscle strength, 47
counseling, 50
County Office of Education (COE), 70, 156
county offices of education, 4
COVID-19: distance learning with, 45, 48, 58, 72, 87, 95, 100, 106, 111; pandemic, 42, 58, 74, 76, 83, 85, 87, 95, 106, 111, 113, 120, 126, 129, 141, 167
credentialed education specialist, 164
Crenshaw, Kimberlé, 30
critical disability education studies, 38
critical race theory (CRT), 25, 30–31

186 ▪ INDEX

cross-pollination, of frameworks, 29
CRP. *See* culturally relevant pedagogy
CRT. *See* critical race theory
CSP. *See* culturally sustaining pedagogy
cultural anthropology, 11
cultural background, 24
cultural barriers, 41
cultural competence, 25
cultural humility, 6, 15, 24–25, 139
culturally and linguistically diverse (CLD) families, 3, 8, 159–60; accessibility for, 9; experiences of, 10, 41; parental engagement of, 15–17; parents, 10; perspectives and experiences of, 22–24
culturally relevant pedagogy (CRP), 25
culturally sustaining pedagogy (CSP), 15, 25–26
cultural otherness, 16
culture: dominant, 33; immigrants, 128; mismatch, 4, 128; of possibility, 32; students and, 8–9
customs, 141

de-escalation techniques, 91
deficit notion of disability, 36–37
DELAC. *See* District English Learner Advisory Council
depression, 12, 38, 96, 109
DI. *See* differentiated instruction
Diagnostic and Statistical Manual of Mental Disorders (*DSM*), 79
dialogues, 166–67; parent protocol, 173
differentiated instruction (DI), 153
disability, 144; born with, 3; childhood, 3; critical disability education studies, 38; cultural views of, 36; deficit notion of, 36–37; historical background, 6–8; ID, 111; intersectional study of, 37; LD, 22, 129; multiple, 83; rights for parents, 4; SLD, 45, 56, 58, 65, 70, 98, 131; social model of, 36; societal views of, 36; in United States, 6–8; values-based, 38, 145
Disability Studies in Education (DSE), 4, 13, 139; anatomy, 36–39; application, 38–39; in education, 34–35, 142–45; foundational, 36–37, 143–44; interdisciplinary, 37, 144; lineage, 35; participatory, 37–38, 144; social, 36, 143; values based, 38, 145
Disability Studies Quarterly, 35
Disability Visibility, 37
District English Learner Advisory Council (DELAC), 9
district-level planning, 120
diversity, 68, 110, 148
DNQ. *See* does not qualify
documented status, 37, 144, 157
does not qualify (DNQ), 52, 77, 131
DSE. *See* Disability Studies in Education
DSM. *See Diagnostic and Statistical Manual of Mental Disorders*
due process, 19, 55
dyslexia, 68, 129, 132–33

EAHCA. *See* Education for All Handicapped Children Act
early childhood development, 77
early intervention (EI), 67, 86, 102, 122, 131
ear tubes, 97
echolalia, 46
ED. *See* emotional disturbance
education: access to, 6; bilingual, 9; disability studies in, 34–35, 142–45; beyond high school, 32; importance of, 32; inclusive, 38; leadership, 4; system, 5
Educationally Related Mental Health Services (ERMHS), 72–73
Education Code, 103
Education for All Handicapped Children Act (EAHCA), 7
Education of the Handicapped Act (EHA), 7
EI. *See* early intervention
Eiko and James, 50–56
ELAC. *See* English Learner Advisory Council; English Learning Advisory Committee
Elementary and Secondary Education Act (ESEA), 7; Title VII, 8

ELL. *See* English language learners
elopement, of students, 51, 80–81, 103
emancipatory pedagogy, 25
emancipatory praxis, 13
Emily, 45–50
emotional disturbance (ED), 65, 95–98
emotional needs, 124
empathy, 147
English immersion programs, 9
English language learners (ELL), 9
English Learner Advisory Council (ELAC), 9
English Learning Advisory Committee (ELAC), 134
English only (EO) students, 9
equitable opportunities, 156
equity, 9, 38, 146
ERMHS. *See* Educationally Related Mental Health Services
ESEA. *See* Elementary and Secondary Education Act
ESSA. *See* Every Student Succeeds Act
ethical responsibility, 9
ethnicity, 63, *163*
ethnocentric values, 16
Every Student Succeeds Act (ESSA), 8
exclusion, 38
extended family, 32

Facilitated Individualized Education Plan (FIEP), 154
familial capital, 29, 32, 141
families, centering of: moving forward by, 156–57
Family Educational Rights and Privacy Act (FERPA), 108
FAPE. *See* free, appropriate, public education
FBA. *See* functional behavioral assessment
federal aid, for schools, 7
federal funding, 8
FERPA. *See* Family Educational Rights and Privacy Act
fidgets, 49
FIEP. *See* Facilitated Individualized Education Plan
5150 psychiatric hold, 98

financial literacy, 32
financial stability, 32
First Five California, 77
focus groups, 167; protocol, 173–74
foundational disability, 36–37; studies, 143–44
free, appropriate, public education (FAPE), 7, 55, 104
freedom, 6
functional behavioral assessment (FBA), 81

Gallaudet, Thomas Hopkins, 6
Gallaudet University, 7
gender, 6, 37, 101, 144, 157; diverse students, 108; expression, 108; identity, 105, 108
GGRC. *See* Golden Gate Regional Center
global pandemic, 58. *See also* COVID-19
Gloria and Tony, 74–83
Golden Gate Regional Center (GGRC), 78, 113
grounded theory, 43; approach to, 161
growth mindset, 139

harassment, 105
hearing loss, temporary, 97
heritage, 73
Hill Collins, Patricia, 30
homeschool, 135
hybrid learning, 106

ID. *See* intellectual disability
IDEA. *See* Individuals with Disabilities Education Act
IEP. *See* Individualized Education Plan
IFSP. *See* Individualized Family Service Plan
immersion school, 115
immigrants: culture, 128; parents, 16; undocumented, 9
implicit bias, 49, 147
impulsivity, 51
inclusion, 93, 119; in education, 38
Individualized Education Plan (IEP), 7, 86; depersonalization in, 23;

document readability, 4; drafts prior to meeting, 150; as legal document, 3; meetings, 16, 74, 88–89; parent statement in, 55; process, 4, 10; team members, 18; teams, 151–52; templates, 155; translation and linguistic needs for, 4; triennial evaluation, 48
Individualized Family Service Plan (IFSP), 86, 114
Individuals with Disabilities Education Act (IDEA), 4, 8, 108, 115; federal funding for, 18; mandates of, 17
Individuals with Disabilities Education Act (IDEA) reauthorization of 2004, 4
inequity, in power, 30; challenge of, 33
institutional racism, 49, 73
intellectual disability (ID), 111
interdisciplinary disability, 37; studies, 144
intergenerational knowledge, 141
interpreters, 5, 17, 20, 43, 56, 84, 92
intersectional study of disability, 37
introduction, 3–5, 12–13; culturally and linguistically diverse students, 8–9; historical background on disability and special education in United States, 6–8; research purpose and significance, 9–11

Judi, 111–21
juvenile detention facilities, 69

labor unions, 153
Ladson-Billings, Gloria, 11
languages, 8, 33, *154*; ASL, 85; barriers, 16; bilingual, 100, 115, 156; ELL, 9; nonverbal, 147; preference, 157; skills, 140; trilingual, 50
Larry P. decision of 1979, 132
LatCrit framework, 30
Latinx peoples, 30
Lau v. Nichols, 9
LCAP. *See* local control accountability plan process
LD. *See* learning disability
learning conditions, optimal, 138
learning disability (LD), 22, 129

LEAs. *See* local education agencies
least restrictive environment (LRE), 7, 82, 115, 136
Legal Aid, 56, 60–61; services, 20
legal compliance, 9, 145
legal representation, 104
LEP. *See* limited English proficiency
lesson pacing, 137
Leticia, 56–60
Lewin, Kurt, 165
LGBTQIA+ spectrum, 25, 110
lifelong learning, 25
limited English proficiency (LEP), 9
linguistic capital, 29, 33, 140–41
linguistics, 8–9
Lisa, 95–100
literature review, 28; communication and collaboration, 20–21; compliance, 17–19; cultural humility, 24–25; culturally sustaining pedagogy, 25–26; gap in, 26–27; litigation, 19–20; parental engagement of CLD families, 15–17; perspectives and experiences of CLD families, 22–24; staff development, 21–22
litigation, 19–20, 154
local control accountability plan (LCAP) process, 9
local education agencies (LEAs), 17–18
LRE. *See* least restrictive environment
lunch bunch groups, 152

mainstreaming, of students, 93, 119
manifest determination (MD), 103, 165
Marxist theory, 36
MD. *See* manifest determination; multiple disability
mediation, 19
medical model, 36, 145
meltdowns, 97, 123–24
mental illness, 109
methodology: collaborators, 165–66; instruments and data collection, 166–67; research design, 160–63; research questions, 159–60; setting, *163*, 163–65, *164*; strengths and limitations/trustworthiness, 167–68

Mia, 165
microaggressions, 33
microcephaly, 84
migratory communities, 17
mindsets: assess-based, 6; growth, 139
Mi Padre, 23
monolingual families, 16
Moore, Liz, 36
Morse code, 85
multigeneous communities, 27
multiple disability (MD), 83
multisensory approach, to learning, 21
music therapy, 125

narrative inquiry summary, 137–39
National Deaf-Mute College, 7
National Institute of Adult Literacy, 4
navigational capital, 29, 33–34, 141–42
networking, 141
nonbinary, 95, 101, 105, 107
nonpublic school (NPS), 12, 69, 95, 104
nonverbal, 85
"Notice of Procedural Safeguards," 4, 61, 74, 154, *154*
NPS. *See* nonpublic school
nuclear family, 32
nursing, 164

Obama, Michelle, 73
occupational therapist, 77
occupational therapy (OT): assessment, 54, 118, 124; frustration with, 117; through insurance, 46–47; from outside provider, 45; school-based, 49, 61; services, 65, 68, 87, 99, 105, 113, 164
OCR. *See* Office of Civil Rights
ODD. *See* oppositional defiant disorder
Office of Civil Rights (OCR), 9, 19, 104
OHI. *See* other health impairment
O&M. *See* orientation and mobility
open-coded dialogue transcripts, 43
oppositional defiant disorder (ODD), 97
orientation and mobility (O&M), 164
OT. *See* occupational therapy
other health impairment (OHI), 45, 65, 70

otherness, 143
outside providers, 47, 62

PAR. *See* participatory action research
paraeducator, 48
parent: as advocate, 137, 148–49; dialogue protocol, 173; interviews, 41–43; perspectives, disregard of, 137, 147–48; support groups, 21, 62, 74
parental consent, 159
parental engagement, issues in: introduction to, 3–13; literature review, 15–28; parental involvement and, 15; theoretical frameworks, 29–40
parent-led groups, 17
parent narratives, 41–43, *43*; dialogue protocol, 173–74; Emily, Eiko and James, and Leticia, 45–64; Judi, Aida, and Rachel, 111–36; Lisa and Vanessa, 95–110; methodology, 159–68; possibilities, 137–58; Roger, Gloria and Tony, and Tomas, 65–94
parent-teacher association (PTA), 62, 100, 134
parent-teacher organization (PTO), 134
participatory action research (PAR), 161
participatory disability, 37–38; studies, 144
PD. *See* professional development
PDF. *See* portable document format
peer: friends, 152; relationships, 69
physical impairments, 84
physical restraint, 91
physical therapy (PT), 84, 99, 105, 164
PL 94-142, 7
PLCs. *See* professional learning communities
portable document format (PDF), 74
positionality, 11–13
positive learning environment, 91
possibilities: aspirational capital, 140; assets-based thinking, 139, 149; case managers, 150–51; CCW, 140; collective problem-solving, 149; convenience of educator/school/

district, 146–74; disability studies in education, 142–45; disregard of parent perspectives, 147–48; familial capital, 141; foundational disability studies, 143–44; IEP teams, 151–52; interdisciplinary disability studies, 144; linguistic capital, 140–41; moving forward by centering families, 156–57; narrative inquiry summary, 137–39; navigational capital, 141–42; parent as advocate, 148–49; participatory disability studies, 144; recommendations and, 150; resistant capital, 142; school boards and labor unions, 153; school districts, 153–54; SELPA, *154*, 154–55; site administrators, 152; social capital, 141; social disability studies, 143; special education departments, 152–53; state department of education, 155; study implications, 156; themes through educator lens, 145–46; theoretical frameworks findings, 139–40; values based disability studies, 145
post-dialogue reflection, 61–63, 90–93, 109–10, 135–36
power, inequity of, 30
preferential seating, 47
private school, 127, 133
privilege, 63, 121, 141, 143
proactive planning, 120
professional development (PD), 19, 21
professional learning communities (PLCs), 22
program specialist, 50
prone restraint, prolonged, 91
pronouns, 101, 105, 108
Proposition 58, 9
Proposition 187 in 1994, 9
Proposition 227 in 1998, 9
proprioceptive input, 49
psychoeducational assessment, 51, 53, 57
psychologist, school, 3, 52, 77
PT. *See* physical therapy
PTA. *See* parent-teacher association
PTO. *See* parent-teacher organization

public education, 25
public school districts, 4

questioning, 162

race, 6, 27–30, 37, 63, 144, 157, *163*
Rachel, 128–34
racial background, 24
racism, 30; institutional, 49, 73
reading ability: of American adults, 4–5; postsecondary, 5
reading intervention services, 68
reflecting, 162
release of information (ROI), 47
religion, 37
research: American Education Research Association, 35; collaborative action, 161; design, 160–63; PAR, 161; purpose and significance, 9–11; questions, 159–60
resistant capital, 29, 33, 142
resources, 31; fight for, 107; lack of, 4
resource specialist (RSP), 45–50, 58, 65, 71, 102, 121, 132
resource specialist program (RSP), 165
restraint: in schools, 91; training, 12
Rice, Tamir, 103–4
Roger, 65–74
ROI. *See* release of information
"rolling narratives," 149
RSP. *See* resource specialist; resource specialist program

SAI. *See* specialized academic instruction
San Mateo County Pride Center, 108
school: based services, 90; boards, 153; districts, 153–54; suspension, 103
school improvement plan (SIP), 22
school site council (SSC), 134
School Success and Opportunity Act (AB 1266), 108
SCIA. *See* Special Circumstance Instructional Assistance
SDCs. *See* special day classes
SEAs. *See* state education agencies
seclusion, in schools, 91, 105
Section 504 plan, 108, 132

SEDAC. *See* Special Education District Advisory Council
segregation, of students, 143
SEIS. *See* Special Education Information System
self-advocacy skills, 17
self-esteem, 71
self-evaluation, 24
self-harm statements, 98, 100
SELPAs. *See* special education local planning areas
semi-structured empathy protocol, 42
sensory: disorder, 84; integration, 47; items, 49; multisensory approach, to learning, 21; needs, 124; overstimulation, 80; seeking input, 45
sexual identity, 157
sexuality, 144
sexual orientation, 37
SIP. *See* school improvement plan
site administrators, 152
SLD. *See* specific learning disability
SLI. *See* speech and language impairment
SLP. *See* speech language pathologist
social capital, 29, 32, 141
social disability, 36; studies, 143
social groups, 71
social justice, 4, 35, 38, 146
social model of disability, 36
social skills group, 52
social status, 6
societal oppression, 4
socioeconomic status, 148, 157
sociology, 35
"soft academic" classes, 121
Special Circumstance Instructional Assistance (SCIA), 86, 121, 164
special day classes (SDCs), 18, 51, 70, 76, 80–83, 98, 114, 121
special education: assessment, 68; attorney, 104; departments, 152–53; eligibility, 3; funding for, 4–5; historical background, 6–8; laws and mandates, 52, 100; multidisciplinary teams, 3; support teams, 4; teams, 11;
triennial reevaluation, 45; in United States, 6–8
Special Education District Advisory Council (SEDAC), 17, 50, 74, 100, 152
Special Education Information System (SEIS), 74, 155
special education local planning areas (SELPAs), 4, *154*, 154–55
specialized academic instruction (SAI), 50, 72, 104–5, 164
specific learning disability (SLD), 45, 56, 58, 65, 70, 98, 131
speech: language evaluation and, 51, 53, 57; SLI, 46, 50, 53, 58, 65, 74, 95, 98, 102, 111, 121; SLP, 45, 48, 68, 77, 117; therapy, 45, 65, 68, 99, 105, 164; to-text accommodations, 59
speech and language impairment (SLI), 46. *See also* speech
speech language pathologist (SLP), 45. *See also* speech
SSC. *See* school site council
SST. *See* student study team; student success team
staff: bilingual, 153; communication with, 48, 116; development, 21–22; shortages, 117
standardized testing, 107
state department of education, 155
state education agencies (SEAs), 17
stigma, 6, 97, 132
structural functional epistemology, 143
structural functionalism, 146
students: of color, 8; culturally and linguistically diverse, 8–9; demographics, *164*
student study team (SST), 164
student success team (SST), 57
suicidal statements, 100
support group, 50; parent, 21, 62, 74
systemic barriers, 4, 41

TDC. *See* therapeutic day class
teacher-parent relationship, 140
text-to-speech accommodations, 59
themes, through educator lens, 145–46

theoretical frameworks: application, 34, 38–39; aspirational capital, 32; CCW, 29; CCW anatomy, 31; CCW lineage, 30–31; cross-pollination of, 29; disability studies anatomy, 36–39; disability studies in education, 34–35; disability studies lineage, 35; familial capital, 32; findings, 139–40; foundational disability study, 36–37; interdisciplinary disability study, 37; linguistic capital, 33; navigational capital, 33–34; participatory disability study, 37–38; resistant capital, 33; social capital, 32; social disability study, 36; values-based disability study, 38
therapeutic day class (TDC or TSDC), 12, 69
Title IX of the Education Amendments Act of 1972, 108
Title VII of the ESEA (Elementary and Secondary Education Act), 9
TK. *See* transitional kindergarten
Tomas, 83–90
traditions, 141
transgender, 108
transitional kindergarten (TK), 51
translators, 5
trust, 80, 138, 168
TSDC. *See* therapeutic day class

UDL. *See* universal design for learning
"ugly laws," 6
Union of the Physically Impaired Against Segregation, 36
universal design for learning (UDL), 26, 153
upward mobility, 32

values-based disability, 38; studies, 145
Vanessa, 100–108
vision: impairment, 85, 130; services, 164

Weber Bill, 91
weighted vest, 49
White supremacy, 8
Wong, Alice, 37

yoga balls, 49
Yosso, Tara, 30

Zola, Irving, 35

About the Author

Kristin Vogel-Campbell, EdD (she/her/hers), has twenty years of experience in special education. She began her career as a special education aide at the Chinatown Head Start in New York City and has taught in a variety of settings in California with students ages five through fourteen. She has served as a district-level program specialist, director of special education, and is currently a coordinator of special education for the San Mateo Foster City School District in Northern California. Dr. Vogel-Campbell serves on the advisory board of two education and human rights nonprofits in the San Francisco Bay Area. This is her first book.